NOTABLE ECONOMISTS

ECONOMICS
TAKING THE MYSTERY OUT OF MONEY

NOTABLE ECONOMISTS

EDITED BY BRIAN DUIGNAN,
SENIOR EDITOR, RELIGION AND PHILOSOPHY

Britannica®
Educational Publishing

IN ASSOCIATION WITH

ROSEN
EDUCATIONAL SERVICES

Published in 2013 by Britannica Educational Publishing
(a trademark of Encyclopædia Britannica, Inc.)
in association with Rosen Educational Services, LLC
29 East 21st Street, New York, NY 10010.

Copyright © 2013 Encyclopædia Britannica, Inc. Britannica, Encyclopædia Britannica, and the Thistle logo are registered trademarks of Encyclopædia Britannica, Inc. All rights reserved.

Rosen Educational Services materials copyright © 2013 Rosen Educational Services, LLC. All rights reserved.

Distributed exclusively by Rosen Educational Services.
For a listing of additional Britannica Educational Publishing titles, call toll free (800) 237-9932.

First Edition

Britannica Educational Publishing
J.E. Luebering: Senior Manager
Adam Augustyn: Assistant Manager
Marilyn L. Barton: Senior Coordinator, Production Control
Steven Bosco: Director, Editorial Technologies
Lisa S. Braucher: Senior Producer and Data Editor
Yvette Charboneau: Senior Copy Editor
Kathy Nakamura: Manager, Media Acquisition
Brian Duignan, Senior Editor, Religion and Philosophy

Rosen Educational Services
Nicholas Croce: Editor
Nelson Sá: Art Director
Cindy Reiman: Photography Manager
Brian Garvey: Designer, Cover Design
Introduction by John Strazzabosco

Library of Congress Cataloging-in-Publication Data

Notable economists/edited by Brian Duignan.—1st ed.
  p. cm.—(Economics : taking the mystery out of money)
"In association with Britannica Educational Publishing, Rosen Educational Services."
Includes bibliographical references and index.
ISBN 978-1-61530-891-0 (library binding)
1. Economics. 2. Economists. I. Duignan, Brian.
HB76.N688 2013
330.092'2—dc23

2012020470

Manufactured in the United States of America

On the cover: Economist Paul Krugman at a press conference for receiving the Nobel Prize in 2008. *Jeff Zelevansky/Getty Images*

Cover and interior background image zphoto/Shutterstock

3 1327 00587 6800

CONTENTS

Introduction   x

Ch. 1   Adam Smith   1
         Early Life   1
         Glasgow   2
             The Theory of Moral Sentiments   3
         Travels on the Continent   4
             The Wealth of Nations   5
         Society and the "Invisible Hand"   7
Ch. 2   David Ricardo   9
             Laissez-Faire   10
Ch. 3   Karl Marx   14
         Early Years   14
         Brussels Period   18
         Early Years in London   20
         Role in the First International   21
         Last Years   23
Ch. 4   Léon Walras   24
Ch. 5   William Stanley Jevons   26
Ch. 6   Carl Menger   28
Ch. 7   Alfred Marshall   30
Ch. 8   Eugen von Böhm-Bawerk   32
Ch. 9   Friedrich von Wieser   34
Ch. 10   Knut Wicksell   35
Ch. 11   Thorstein Veblen   36
         Early Life   36
         Later Works and Career   38

	Technocracy	39
	Final Years and Assessment	39
Ch. 12	John Rogers Commons	41
Ch. 13	Wesley Clair Mitchell	43
Ch. 14	Arthur Cecil Pigou	45
Ch. 15	John Maynard Keynes	47
	Background and Early Career	47
	Key Contributions	50
	Deficit Financing	51
	Later Works	51
Ch. 16	Ragnar Frisch	53
Ch. 17	Gunnar Myrdal	55
Ch. 18	Bertil Ohlin	57
Ch. 19	Friedrich August von Hayek	59
	Welfare State	61
Ch. 20	Edward Hastings Chamberlin	64
Ch. 21	Sir Roy Harrod	66
Ch. 22	Simon Kuznets	67
Ch. 23	Theodore William Schultz	69
Ch. 24	Jan Tinbergen	71
Ch. 25	Sir John Richard Hicks	73
Ch. 26	Wassily Leontief	74
Ch. 27	James Edward Meade	76
Ch. 28	John Kenneth Galbraith	78
Ch. 29	Tjalling Charles Koopmans	80
Ch. 30	Ronald Coase	82
Ch. 31	George Joseph Stigler	84

Ch. 32	Maurice Allais	85
Ch. 33	Trygve Haavelmo	87
Ch. 34	Leonid Vitalyevich Kantorovich	88
Ch. 35	Milton Friedman	90
	Money Supply	91
Ch. 36	Sir Richard Stone	94
Ch. 37	William Vickrey	95
Ch. 38	Sir Arthur Lewis	97
Ch. 39	Paul Samuelson	98
Ch. 40	Herbert Alexander Simon	100
Ch. 41	Leonid Hurwicz	102
Ch. 42	James Tobin	104
Ch. 43	Franco Modigliani	106
Ch. 44	James McGill Buchanan	108
Ch. 45	John Charles Harsanyi	109
Ch. 46	Lawrence Robert Klein	111
Ch. 47	Douglass Cecil North	113
Ch. 48	Thomas Crombie Schelling	114
Ch. 49	Gerard Debreu	116
Ch. 50	Kenneth Joseph Arrow	117
Ch. 51	Merton Howard Miller	119
Ch. 52	Robert Merton Solow	121
Ch. 53	Robert William Fogel	123
Ch. 54	Vernon Smith	125
Ch. 55	Harry Markowitz	127
Ch. 56	John Forbes Nash, Jr	129
Ch. 57	Robert Aumann	131

Ch. 58	Reinhard Selten	133
Ch. 59	Gary Stanley Becker	134
Ch. 60	Oliver Eaton Williamson	136
Ch. 61	Robert Alexander Mundell	138
Ch. 62	Amartya Sen	140
	Infant Mortality	143
Ch. 63	Edmund Strother Phelps	144
Ch. 64	Elinor Ostrom	146
Ch. 65	Daniel Kahneman	148
Ch. 66	William Forsyth Sharpe	150
Ch. 67	Clive Granger	152
Ch. 68	Sir James Alexander Mirrlees	154
Ch. 69	Daniel Little McFadden	156
Ch. 70	Robert Emerson Lucas, Jr	158
Ch. 71	Dale Mortensen	160
Ch. 72	Peter Arthur Diamond	162
Ch. 73	George Akerlof	164
Ch. 74	Edward Prescott	166
Ch. 75	Myron Samuel Scholes	168
Ch. 76	Christopher Albert Sims	170
Ch. 77	Robert Engle	172
Ch. 78	Michael Spence	174
Ch. 79	Joseph Stiglitz	175
Ch. 80	Thomas John Sargent	177
Ch. 81	Finn Erling Kydland	180
Ch. 82	James Joseph Heckman	182
Ch. 83	Robert Merton	184
Ch. 84	Christopher Antoniou Pissarides	186

Ch. 85 Eric Stark Maskin   188
Ch. 86 Roger Bruce Myerson   190
Ch. 87 Paul Robin Krugman   192

Glossary   194
For Further Reading   197
Index   199

INTRODUCTION

To locate a seminal moment in time, with some measure of coincidence, the science of economics shares the year of its published origins, in the United Kingdom, with that of the birth of the United States of America: 1776. Adam Smith had 17 years earlier written a book called *The Theory of Moral Sentiments*, which attracted the attention of Charles Townshend, who later served as Britain's chancellor of the Exchequer. Impressed, Townshend hired Smith to tutor his stepson, which Smith did for a number of years and at a lucrative stipend. Townshend's decision as chancellor of the Exchequer to impose new import duties on the American colonies contributed to hostilities that eventually led to revolution, and America became an independent nation in the same year that Smith published *An Inquiry into the Nature and Causes of the Wealth of Nations*.

In Britain the publication of Smith's groundbreaking book ushered in a new way of thinking about the dynamics and coordinative processes of capitalism. Smith envisioned people trying to better themselves, which led to competition, which would drive prices to what he saw as natural levels. Thus did the "invisible hand" regulating the economy show itself.

The value of unimpeded access to information is seen in the example of economist Léon Walras (1834–1910). His story also ends with some measure of disappointment. Walras's *Elements of Pure Economics* elaborated one of the original comprehensive mathematical analyses of economic equilibrium, or the state of balance between economic forces such as supply and demand.

He had genuinely innovative ideas, and nowadays his work would have permeated economic scholarship through the Internet. But back then, Walras had another

INTRODUCTION

problem. His book was written in French, while all major economic theorizing was taking place in Britain. Walras received little recognition in his time because the English-speaking public was not exposed to his work in translation. As the chapter on him points out, Walras is now, along with David Ricardo and Karl Marx, one of the most widely studied economists of his era.

Gary S. Becker (1992 Nobel Prize) applied the methods of economics to the study of human behaviour in

Paul Krugman (Left) received the Nobel Prize in Economic Sciences from Carl XVI Gustaf of Sweden in Stockholm on December 10, 2008. Olivier Morin/AFP/Getty Images

realms beyond the scope of conventional economics, including the family. His main thesis was that most aspects of human behaviour are governed by self-interest.

One is drawn to wonder from where in the tortured mind of John Nash (1994 Nobel Prize) any major economic contributions might have come. He suffered from and was hospitalized for schizophrenia. Nash's contribution to the field of mathematics known as game theory found practical application in the decision making of business strategists. Called the Nash equilibrium, his theory explained the dynamics of threat and action among competitors.

Myron S. Scholes (1997 Nobel Prize) helped create the Scholes-Black formula, which provided a means of determining the future value of an option (a contractual agreement enabling the holder to buy or sell a security, such as a stock, at a designated price for a specified period of time). This made options trading more accessible, which in turn greatly expanded the whole field of investment. Scholes shared his prize with Robert C. Merton, who applied the Scholes-Black formula to other areas of finance, such as mortgages and student loans and risk-management assessment, eventually helping to create new investment vehicles.

One might assume that economics is a cold and impersonal discipline, focused solely upon the study of wealth. However, economist Amartya Sen (1998 Nobel Prize), referred to by his contemporaries in the field as the "conscience of his profession," changed that perception. Sen's work in welfare economics focused on the problems of society's poorest members, and his study of the causes of famine led to practical measures for relieving food crises in developing countries.

INTRODUCTION

Research by George A. Akerlof, Joseph E. Stiglitz, and A. Michael Spence (2001 Nobel Prize) shed light on the operation of markets characterized by "asymmetric information," a state in which parties to a transaction have unequal amounts of relevant information. Akerlof concentrated on markets in which sellers of a product have more information about the product's quality than buyers, as in the market for used cars. Stiglitz studied the insurance market, in which insurance companies lack reliable information on the risk factors of their customers. And Spence developed a theory that explained how better-informed individuals convey relevant information to others through "signals"—thus, a job applicant's college degree signals intelligence and ability to prospective employers.

Daniel Kahneman's (2002 Nobel Prize) groundbreaking research refuted the conventional assumption that people attempt to maximize expected utility in their economic decision making when the outcomes of alternative courses of action are uncertain. Instead, they rely on heuristics, or rules of thumb. Kahneman shared his prize with Vernon L. Smith, who developed the use of laboratory experiments in economic analysis.

If you need employment and are wondering how much effort you should put into job seeking, the research of economist Christopher A. Pissarides (2010 Nobel Prize) offers some interesting findings. He determined that the more intensely job seekers look for employment, the more jobs are offered. Pissarides was applying the theory of "friction within search markets," which refers to the resistance between buyers and sellers in finding each other. The perhaps unexpected finding—that the number of jobs offered actually increases as the number of applicants increases—is explained by the fact that the business sector becomes aware of the ease with which it can fill positions. Pissarides shared his prize with Peter A. Diamond and Dale T. Mortensen, who also contributed to the theory of search frictions.

Thomas J. Sargent (2011 Nobel Prize) developed a method for identifying the macroeconomic effects of changes in economic policy, isolating them from the effects that result from private-sector decisions undertaken in rational expectation of changes in economic policy. Sargent shared his prize with Christopher A. Sims, who studied the macroeconomic effects of unexpected economic events.

This volume profiles 87 of the world's most influential economists. Through their achievements we observe the chronological development of economics as a science and the economic modernization of our world.

CHAPTER ONE

Adam Smith

(baptized June 5, 1723, Kirkcaldy, Fife, Scotland—
d. July 17, 1790, Edinburgh)

Adam Smith, a Scottish social philosopher and political economist, is a towering figure in the history of economic thought. Known primarily for a single work—*An Inquiry into the Nature and Causes of the Wealth of Nations* (1776), the first comprehensive system of political economy—Smith is more properly regarded as a social philosopher whose economic writings constitute only the capstone to an overarching view of political and social evolution.

EARLY LIFE

Much more is known about Adam Smith's thought than about his life. Of Smith's childhood nothing is known other than that he received his elementary schooling in Kirkcaldy and that at the age of four years he was said to have been carried off by gypsies. Pursuit was mounted, and young Adam was abandoned by his captors. "He would have made, I fear, a poor gypsy," commented his principal biographer.

At the age of 14, in 1737, Smith entered the University of Glasgow, already remarkable as a centre of what was to become known as the Scottish Enlightenment. Graduating in 1740, Smith won a scholarship and traveled on horseback to Oxford, where he stayed at Balliol College. His years there were spent largely in self-education, from which Smith obtained a firm grasp of both classical and contemporary philosophy.

Returning to his home after an absence of six years, Smith gave a series of public lectures in Edinburgh. The lectures, which ranged over a wide variety of subjects from rhetoric to history and economics, resulted in his appointment in 1751, at the age of 27, as professor of logic at Glasgow, from which post he transferred in 1752 to the more remunerative professorship of moral philosophy, a subject that embraced the related fields of natural theology, ethics, jurisprudence, and political economy.

GLASGOW

Smith then entered upon a period of extraordinary creativity, combined with a social and intellectual life that he afterward described as "by far the happiest, and most honourable period of my life." Among his wide circle of acquaintances were not only members of the aristocracy, many connected with the government, but also a range of intellectual and scientific figures that included the philosopher David Hume, a lifelong friend whom Smith had met in Edinburgh. Smith was also introduced during these years to the company of the great merchants who were carrying on the colonial trade that had opened

Adam Smith, paste medallion by James Tassie, 1787; in the Scottish National Portrait Gallery, Edinburgh. Courtesy of the Scottish National Portrait Gallery, Edinburgh

to Scotland following its union with England in 1707. One of them, Andrew Cochrane, had been a provost of Glasgow and had founded the famous Political Economy Club. From Cochrane and his fellow merchants Smith undoubtedly acquired the detailed information concerning trade and business that was to give such a sense of the real world to *The Wealth of Nations*.

THE THEORY OF MORAL SENTIMENTS

In 1759 Smith published his first work, *The Theory of Moral Sentiments*. In it he described the principles of "human nature," which, together with Hume and the other leading philosophers of his time, he took as a universal and unchanging datum from which social institutions, as well as social behaviour, could be deduced.

One problem in particular interested Smith: the source of the ability to form moral judgments, including judgments on one's own behaviour, in the face of the seemingly overriding passions for self-preservation and self-interest. Smith's answer, at considerable length, is the presence within each of us of an "inner man" who plays the role of the "impartial spectator," approving or condemning our own and others' actions with a voice impossible to disregard.

The thesis of the impartial spectator, however, conceals a more important aspect of the book. Smith saw humans as creatures driven by passions and at the same time self-regulated by their ability to reason and—no less important—by their capacity for sympathy. This duality serves both to pit individuals against one another and to provide them with the rational and moral faculties to create institutions by which the internecine struggle can be mitigated and even turned to the common good. He wrote in his *Moral Sentiments* the famous observation that he was to repeat later in *The Wealth of Nations*: that self-seeking men are often "led by an invisible hand… without knowing it, without intending it, [to] advance the interest of the society."

TRAVELS ON THE CONTINENT

Moral Sentiments quickly brought Smith wide esteem and in particular attracted the attention of Charles Townshend, whose fate it was to be the chancellor of the Exchequer responsible for the measures of taxation that ultimately provoked the American Revolution. Townshend had recently married and was searching for a tutor for his stepson and ward, the young duke of Buccleuch. Influenced by the strong recommendations of Hume and his own admiration for *The Theory of Moral Sentiments*, he approached Smith to take the charge.

The terms of employment were lucrative (an annual salary of £300 plus traveling expenses and a pension of £300 a year thereafter), considerably more than Smith had earned as a professor. Accordingly, Smith resigned his Glasgow post in 1763 and set off for France the next year as the tutor of the young duke. They stayed mainly in Toulouse, where Smith began working on a book (eventually to be *The Wealth of Nations*) as an antidote to the excruciating boredom of the provinces. After 18 months of ennui he was rewarded with a two-month sojourn in Geneva, where he met Voltaire, for whom he had the profoundest respect, thence to Paris, where Hume, then secretary to the British embassy,

introduced Smith to the great literary salons of the French Enlightenment. There he met a group of social reformers and theorists headed by François Quesnay who called themselves *les économistes* but are known in history as the physiocrats.

The stay in Paris was cut short by a shocking event. The younger brother of the duke of Buccleuch, who had joined them in Toulouse, took ill and perished despite Smith's frantic ministrations. Smith and his charge immediately returned to London. Smith worked in London until the spring of 1767 with Lord Townshend. Late that year he returned to Kirkcaldy, where the next six years were spent dictating and reworking *The Wealth of Nations*, followed by another stay of three years in London, where the work was finally completed and published in 1776.

THE WEALTH OF NATIONS

Despite its renown as the first great work in political economy, *The Wealth of Nations* is in fact a continuation of the philosophical theme begun in *The Theory of Moral Sentiments*. The ultimate problem to which Smith

Adam Smith, drawing by John Kay, 1790. © Photos.com/Thinkstock addresses himself is how the inner struggle between the passions and the "impartial spectator"—explicated in *Moral Sentiments* in terms of the single individual—works its effects in the larger arena of history itself, both in the long-run evolution of society and in terms of the immediate characteristics of the stage of history typical of Smith's own day.

The answer to this problem enters in Book V, in which Smith outlines the four main stages of organization through which society is impelled, unless blocked by wars, deficiencies of resources, or bad policies of government: the original "rude" state of hunters, a second stage of nomadic agriculture, a third stage of feudal, or manorial, "farming," and a fourth and final stage of commercial interdependence.

It should be noted that each of these stages is accompanied by institutions suited to its needs. For example, in the age of the huntsman, "there is scarce any property…; so there is seldom any established magistrate or any regular administration of justice." With the advent of flocks there emerges a more complex form of social organization, comprising not only "formidable" armies but the central institution of private property with its indispensable buttress of law and order as well. It is the very essence of Smith's thought that he recognized this institution, whose social usefulness he never doubted, as an instrument for the protection of privilege, rather than one to be justified in terms of natural law: "Civil government," he wrote, "so far as it is instituted for the security of property, is in reality instituted for the defence of the rich against the poor, or of those who have some property against those who have none at all." Finally, Smith describes the evolution through feudalism into a stage of society requiring new institutions, such as market-determined rather than guild-determined wages and free rather than government-constrained enterprise. This later became known as laissez-faire capitalism; Smith called it the system of perfect liberty.

SOCIETY AND THE "INVISIBLE HAND"

The theory of historical evolution, although it is perhaps the binding conception of *The Wealth of Nations*, is subordinated within the work itself to a detailed description of how the "invisible hand" actually operates within the commercial, or final, stage of society. This becomes the focus of Books I and II, in which Smith undertakes to elucidate two questions. The first is how a system of perfect liberty, operating under the drives and constraints of human nature and intelligently designed institutions, will give rise to an orderly society. The question, which had already been considerably elucidated by earlier writers, required both an explanation of the underlying orderliness in the pricing of individual commodities and an explanation of the "laws" that regulated the division of the entire "wealth" of the nation (which Smith saw as its annual production of goods and services) among the three great claimant classes—labourers, landlords, and manufacturers.

This orderliness, as would be expected, was produced by the interaction of the two aspects of human nature, its response to its passions and its susceptibility to reason and sympathy. But whereas *The Theory of Moral Sentiments* had relied mainly on the presence of the "inner man" to provide the necessary restraints to private action, in *The Wealth of Nations* one finds an institutional mechanism that acts to reconcile the disruptive possibilities inherent in a blind obedience to the passions alone. This protective mechanism is competition, an arrangement by which the passionate desire for bettering one's condition is turned into a socially beneficial agency by pitting one person's drive for self-betterment against another's.

It is in the unintended outcome of this competitive struggle for self-betterment that the invisible hand regulating the economy shows itself, for Smith explains how mutual vying forces the prices of commodities down to their "natural" levels, which correspond to their costs of production. Moreover, by inducing labour and capital to move from less to more profitable occupations or areas, the competitive mechanism constantly restores prices to these "natural" levels despite short-run aberrations. Finally, by explaining that wages and rents and profits (the constituent parts of the costs of production) are themselves subject to this same discipline of self-interest and competition, Smith not only provided an ultimate rationale for these "natural" prices but also revealed an underlying orderliness in the distribution of income itself among workers, whose recompense was their wages; landlords, whose income was their rents; and manufacturers, whose reward was their profits.

The Wealth of Nations was received with admiration by Smith's wide circle of friends and admirers, although it was by no means an immediate popular success. The work finished, Smith went into semiretirement. The years passed quietly, with several revisions of both major books but with no further publications. He died at the age of 67, full of honours and recognition, and was buried in the churchyard at Canongate with a simple monument stating that Adam Smith, author of *The Wealth of Nations*, lay there.

CHAPTER TWO

DAVID RICARDO

(b. April 18/19, 1772, London, England—
d. September 11, 1823, Gatcombe Park,
Gloucestershire)

David Ricardo was an English economist who gave systematized, classical form to the rising science of economics in the 19th century. His laissez-faire doctrines were typified in his Iron Law of Wages, which stated that all attempts to improve the real income of workers were futile and that wages perforce remained near the subsistence level.

Ricardo was the third son born to a family of Sephardic Jews who had emigrated from the Netherlands to England. At the age of 14 he entered into business with his father, who had made a fortune on the London Stock Exchange. By the time he was 21, however, he had broken with his father over religion, become a Unitarian, and married a Quaker. He continued as a member of the stock exchange, where his talents and character won him the support of an eminent banking house. He did so well that in a few years he acquired a fortune, which allowed him to pursue interests in literature and science, particularly in the fields of mathematics, chemistry, and geology.

David Ricardo, portrait by Thomas Phillips, 1821; in the National Portrait Gallery, London. Courtesy of The National Portrait Gallery, London

LAISSEZ-FAIRE

Laissez-faire (French: "allow to do") is the policy of minimum governmental interference in the economic affairs of individuals and society. The origin of the term is uncertain, but folklore suggests that it is derived from the answer Jean-Baptiste Colbert, controller general of finance under King Louis XIV of France, received when he asked industrialists what the government could do to help business: "Leave us alone." The doctrine of laissez-faire is usually associated with the economists known as physiocrats, who flourished in France from about 1756 to 1778. The policy of laissez-faire received strong support in classical economics as it developed in Great Britain under the influence of economist and philosopher Adam Smith.

Belief in laissez-faire was a popular view during the 19th century; its proponents cited the assumption in classical economics of a natural economic order as support for their faith in unregulated individual activity. The British economist John Stuart Mill was responsible for

John Stuart Mill, carte de visite, 1884. Library of Congress, Washington, D.C. (Neg. Co. LC-USZ62-76491)

bringing this philosophy into popular economic usage in his *Principles of Political Economy* (1848), in which he set forth the arguments for and against government activity in economic affairs.

Laissez-faire was a political as well as an economic doctrine. The pervading theory of the 19th century was that the individual, pursuing his own desired ends, would thereby achieve the best results for the society of which he was a part. The function of the state was to maintain order and security and to avoid interference with the initiative of the individual in pursuit of his own desired goals. But laissez-faire advocates nonetheless argued that government had an essential role in enforcing contracts as well as ensuring civil order.

The philosophy's popularity reached its peak around 1870. In the late 19th century the acute changes caused by industrial growth and the adoption of mass-production techniques proved the laissez-faire doctrine insufficient as a guiding philosophy. Although the original concept yielded to new theories that attracted wider support, the general philosophy still has its advocates.

Ricardo's interest in economic questions arose in 1799 when he read Adam Smith's *Wealth of Nations*. For 10 years he studied economics, somewhat offhandedly at first and then with greater concentration. His first published work was *The High Price of Bullion, a Proof of the Depreciation of Bank Notes* (1810), an outgrowth of letters Ricardo had published in the *Morning Chronicle* the year before.

In 1815 a controversy arose over the Corn Laws, which regulated the import and export of grain. A decline in wheat prices had led Parliament to raise the tariff on imported wheat. This provoked a popular

outcry and caused Ricardo to publish his *Essay on the Influence of a Low Price of Corn on the Profits of Stock* (1815), in which he argued that raising the tariff on grain imports tended to increase the rents of the country gentlemen while decreasing the profits of manufacturers. One year before his Corn Law essay, at the age of 42, he had retired from business and taken up residence in Gloucestershire, where he had extensive landholdings.

Later, in *Principles of Political Economy and Taxation* (1817), Ricardo analyzed the laws determining the distribution of everything that could be produced by the "three classes of the community"—namely, the landlords, the workers, and the owners of capital. As part of his theory of distribution, he concluded that profits vary inversely with wages, which rise or fall in line with the cost of necessities. He also concluded that trade between countries was influenced by relative costs of production and by differences in internal price structures that could maximize the comparative advantages of the trading countries.

David Ricardo. Hulton Archive/Getty Images

In 1819 Ricardo purchased a seat in the House of Commons, as was done in those times, and entered Parliament as a member for Portarlington. He was not a frequent speaker, but so great was his reputation in economic affairs that his opinions on free trade were received with respect, even though they did not represent the dominant thinking in the House. Illness forced Ricardo to retire from Parliament in 1823. He died that year at the age of 51.

Despite his relatively short career and the fact that most of it was preoccupied with business affairs, Ricardo achieved a leading position among the economists of his time. Although his ideas have long since been superseded or modified by other work and by new theoretical approaches, Ricardo retains his eminence as the thinker who first systematized economics. Writers of various persuasions drew heavily upon his ideas, including those who favoured laissez-faire capitalism and those, such as Karl Marx and Robert Owen, who opposed it.

CHAPTER THREE

KARL MARX

(b. May 5, 1818, Trier, Rhine province, Prussia [Germany]—d. March 14, 1883, London, England)

Karl Marx was a revolutionary, sociologist, historian, and economist. He published (with Friedrich Engels) *Manifest der Kommunistischen Partei* (1848), commonly known as *The Communist Manifesto*, the most celebrated pamphlet in the history of the socialist movement. He also was the author of the movement's most important book, *Das Kapital*. These writings and others by Marx and Engels form the basis of the body of thought and belief known as Marxism.

EARLY YEARS

Karl Heinrich Marx was the oldest surviving boy of nine children. Both his parents were Jewish and were descended from a long line of rabbis, but, a year or so before Karl was born, his father—probably because his professional career required it—was baptized in the Evangelical Established Church. Karl was baptized when he was six years old.

Marx was educated from 1830 to 1835 at the high school in Trier. In October 1835 he matriculated at the University of Bonn, and one year later he enrolled at the University of Berlin to study law and philosophy. Marx's crucial experience at Berlin was his introduction

Karl Marx. Courtesy of the trustees of the British Museum; photograph, J.R. Freeman & Co. Ltd.

to George Wilhelm Friedrich Hegel's philosophy, regnant there, and his adherence to the Young Hegelians. At first he felt a repugnance toward Hegel's doctrines. The Hegelian pressure in the revolutionary student culture was powerful, however, and Marx joined a society called the Doctor Club, whose members were intensely involved in the new literary and philosophical movement.

By 1841 the Young Hegelians had become left republicans. Marx's studies, meanwhile, were lagging. Urged by his friends, he submitted a doctoral dissertation to the university at Jena, which was known to be lax in its academic requirements, and received his degree in April 1841.

In 1841 Marx, together with other Young Hegelians, was much influenced by the publication of *Das Wesen des Christentums* (1841; *The Essence of Christianity*) by Ludwig Feuerbach. Its author, to Marx's mind, successfully criticized Hegel, an idealist who believed that matter or existence was inferior to and dependent upon mind or spirit, from the opposite, or materialist, standpoint, showing how the "Absolute Spirit" was a projection of "the real man standing on the foundation of nature." Henceforth Marx's philosophical efforts were toward a combination of Hegel's dialectic—the idea that all things are in a continual process of change resulting from the conflicts between their contradictory aspects—with Feuerbach's materialism, which placed material conditions above ideas.

In October 1842, Marx became editor of the *Rheinische Zeitung*, a liberal democratic organ of a group of young merchants, bankers, and industrialists. Marx succeeded in trebling his newspaper's circulation and making it a leading journal in Prussia. Nevertheless, Prussian authorities suspended it for being too outspoken, and

Marx agreed to coedit with the liberal Hegelian Arnold Ruge a new review, the *Deutsch-französische Jahrbücher* ("German-French Yearbooks"), which was to be published in Paris.

First, however, in June 1843 Marx, after an engagement of seven years, married Jenny von Westphalen. Jenny was an attractive, intelligent, and much-admired woman, four years older than Karl; she came of a family of military and administrative distinction. Four months after their marriage, the young couple moved to Paris, which was then the centre of socialist thought and of the more extreme sects that went under the name of communism. There, Marx first became a revolutionary and a communist and began to associate with communist societies of French and German workingmen. Their ideas were, in his view, "utterly crude and unintelligent," but their character moved him: "The brotherhood of man is no mere phrase with them, but a fact of life, and the nobility of man shines upon us from their work-hardened bodies," he wrote in his so-called "Ökonomisch-philosophische Manuskripte aus dem Jahre 1844" (written in 1844; *Economic and Philosophic Manuscripts of 1844* [1959]).

The "German-French Yearbooks" proved short-lived, but through their publication Marx befriended Friedrich Engels, a contributor who was to become his lifelong collaborator, and in their pages appeared Marx's article "Zur Kritik der Hegelschen Rechtsphilosophie" ("Toward the Critique of the Hegelian Philosophy of Right") with its oft-quoted assertion that religion is the "opium of the people." It was there, too, that he first raised the call for an "uprising of the proletariat" to realize the conceptions of philosophy. Once more, however, the Prussian government intervened against Marx. He was expelled from France and left for Brussels—followed by Engels—in February 1845. That year in Belgium he renounced his Prussian nationality.

BRUSSELS PERIOD

The next two years in Brussels saw the deepening of Marx's collaboration with Engels. Engels had seen at first-hand in Manchester, England, where a branch factory of his father's textile firm was located, all the depressing aspects of the Industrial Revolution. He had also been a Young Hegelian and had been converted to communism by Moses Hess, who was called the "communist rabbi." In England he associated with the followers of Robert Owen. Now he and Marx, finding that they shared the same views, combined their intellectual resources and published *Die heilige Familie* (1845; *The Holy Family*), a prolix criticism of the Hegelian idealism of the theologian Bruno Bauer. Their next work, *Die deutsche Ideologie* (written 1845–46, published 1932; *The German Ideology*), contained the fullest exposition of their important materialistic conception of history, which set out to show how, historically, societies had been structured to promote the interests of the economically dominant class. But it found no publisher and remained unknown during its authors' lifetimes.

An unusual sequence of events led Marx and Engels to write their pamphlet *The Communist Manifesto*. In June 1847 a secret society, the League of the Just, composed mainly of emigrant German handicraftsmen, met in London and decided to formulate a political program. They sent a representative to Marx to ask him to join the league; Marx overcame his doubts and, with Engels, joined the organization, which thereupon changed its name to the Communist League and enacted a democratic constitution. Entrusted with the task of composing their program, Marx and Engels worked from the middle of December 1847 to the end of January 1848. The London Communists were already impatiently threatening Marx with disciplinary action when he sent them the manuscript; they promptly adopted it as their manifesto. It enunciated the proposition that all history had hitherto been a history of class struggles; summarized in pithy form the materialist conception of history worked out in *The German Ideology*; and asserted that the forthcoming victory of the proletariat would put an end to class society forever. It closed with the words, "The proletarians have nothing to lose but their chains. They have a world to win. Workingmen of all countries, unite!"

Revolution suddenly erupted in Europe in the first months of 1848, in France, Italy, and Austria. Marx had been invited to Paris by a member of the provisional government just in time to avoid expulsion by the Belgian government. As the revolution gained in Austria and Germany, Marx returned to the Rhineland. In Cologne he advocated a policy of coalition between the working class and the democratic bourgeoisie. Marx pressed his policy through the pages of the *Neue Rheinische Zeitung* ("New Rhenish Newspaper"), newly founded in June 1849, urging a constitutional democracy and war with Russia. When the king of Prussia dissolved the Prussian Assembly in Berlin, Marx called for arms and men to help the resistance. Bourgeois liberals withdrew their support from Marx's newspaper, and he himself was indicted on several charges, including advocacy of the nonpayment of taxes. In his trial he defended himself with the argument that the crown was engaged in making an unlawful counterrevolution. The jury acquitted him unanimously and with thanks. Nevertheless, Marx was ordered banished as an alien on May 16, 1849. The final issue of his newspaper, printed in red, caused a great sensation.

EARLY YEARS IN LONDON

Expelled once more from Paris, Marx went to London in August 1849. It was to be his home for the rest of his life. Chagrined by the failure of his own tactics of collaboration with the liberal bourgeoisie, he rejoined the Communist League in London and for about a year advocated a bolder revolutionary policy. In 1852 he published, in a German-American periodical, his essay "Der Achtzehnte Brumaire des Louis Napoleon" (*The Eighteenth Brumaire of Louis Bonaparte*), with its acute analysis of the formation of a bureaucratic absolutist state with the support of the peasant class. In other respects the next 12 years were, in Marx's words, years of "isolation" both for him and for Engels in his Manchester factory.

From 1850 to 1864 Marx lived in material misery and spiritual pain. His funds were gone, and except on one occasion he could not bring himself to seek paid employment. In March 1850 he and his wife and four

Karl Marx. Photos.com/Thinkstock

small children were evicted and their belongings seized. Several of his children died. For six years the family lived in two small rooms in Soho, often subsisting on bread and potatoes.

During all these years Engels loyally contributed to Marx's financial support. The sums were not large at first, for Engels was only a clerk in the firm of Ermen and Engels at Manchester. Later, however, in 1864, when he became a partner, his subventions were generous. Marx was proud of Engels's friendship and would tolerate no criticism of him.

In 1859 Marx published his first book on economic theory, *Zur Kritik der politischen Ökonomie* (*A Contribution to the Critique of Political Economy*). In its preface he again summarized his materialistic conception of history, his theory that the course of history is dependent on economic developments. At this time, however, Marx regarded his studies in economic and social history at the British Museum as his main task. He was busy producing the drafts of his magnum opus, which was to be published later as *Das Kapital*.

ROLE IN THE FIRST INTERNATIONAL

Marx's political isolation ended in 1864 with the founding of the International Working Men's Association. Although he was neither its founder nor its head, he soon became its leading spirit. The International grew in prestige and membership, its numbers reaching perhaps 800,000 in 1869. It was successful in several interventions on behalf of European trade unions engaged in struggles with employers.

In 1870, however, Marx was still unknown as a European political personality; it was the Paris Commune that made him into an international figure, "the best calumniated and most menaced man of London," as he wrote. When the Franco-German War broke out in 1870, Marx and Engels disagreed with followers in Germany who refused to vote in the Reichstag in favour of the war. The General Council declared that "on the German side the war was a war of defence." After the defeat of the French armies, however, they felt that the German terms amounted to aggrandizement at the expense of the French people. When an insurrection broke out in Paris and the Paris Commune was proclaimed, Marx gave it his unswerving support.

The advent of the Commune, however, exacerbated the antagonisms within the International Working Men's Association and thus brought about its downfall. English trade unionists such as George Odger, former president of the General Council, opposed Marx's support of the Paris Commune. The Reform Bill of 1867, which had enfranchised the British working class, had opened vast opportunities for political action by the trade unions. English labour leaders found they could make many practical advances by cooperating with the Liberal Party and, regarding Marx's rhetoric as an encumbrance, resented his charge that they had "sold themselves" to the Liberals.

A left opposition also developed under the leadership of the famed Russian revolutionary Mikhail Alexandrovich Bakunin. Bakunin admired Marx's intellect but strongly opposed several of his theories, especially Marx's support of the centralized structure of the International, Marx's view that the proletariat class should act as a political party against prevailing parties but within the existing parliamentary system, and Marx's belief that the proletariat, after it had overthrown the bourgeois state, should establish its own regime. To Bakunin, the mission of the revolutionary was destruction. He acquired followers, mostly young men, in Italy, Switzerland, and France, and he organized a secret society, the International Alliance of Social Democracy, which in 1869 challenged the hegemony of the General Council at the congress in Basel, Switzerland. Marx, however, had already succeeded in preventing its admission as an organized body into the International.

At the congress of the International at The Hague in 1872, the only one he ever attended, Marx managed to defeat the Bakuninists. Then, to the consternation of the delegates, Engels moved that the seat of the General Council be transferred from London to New York City. The Bakuninists were expelled, but the International languished and was finally disbanded in Philadelphia in 1876.

LAST YEARS

During the next and last decade of his life, Marx's creative energies declined. He was beset by what he called "chronic mental depression," and his life turned inward toward his family. He was unable to complete any substantial work, though he still read widely and undertook to learn Russian.

Despite Marx's withdrawal from active politics, he still retained what Engels called his "peculiar influence" on the leaders of working-class and socialist movements. During his last years Marx spent much time at health resorts and even traveled to Algiers. He was broken by the death of his wife on December 2, 1881, and of his eldest daughter, Jenny Longuet, on January 11, 1883. He died in London, evidently of a lung abscess, in the following year.

CHAPTER FOUR

Léon Walras

(b. December 16, 1834, Évreux, France—d. January 5, 1910, Clarens, near Montreux, Switzerland),

The French-born economist Léon Walras is remembered as the author of *Éléments d'économie politique pure* (1874–77; *Elements of Pure Economics*), the first comprehensive mathematical analyses of general economic equilibrium. Because he wrote in French, his work did not get much attention in Britain, the hotbed of 19th-century economics. Today, however, he is among the three most widely studied 19th-century economists, along with Karl Marx and David Ricardo.

After having twice failed the entrance examination to the École Polytechnique in Paris for lack of preparation in mathematics, Walras entered the École des Mines in 1854. Leaving school after a year, he tried literature unsuccessfully. In 1858 his father, the economist Auguste Walras, persuaded him to devote his life to economics. Lacking the necessary formal training, however, Walras could not get a university position. After a brief flirtation with journalism, he worked for several business firms unsuccessfully. Sharing in the popular belief that cooperatives offered an alternative to the revolutionary activity in western Europe, Walras and Léon Say in 1865 began a bank for producers' cooperatives, of which Walras became managing director. The two men also began to publish a monthly journal on cooperatives,

Le travail ("Work"), in 1866. Both the bank and the periodical failed in 1868, but two years later Walras was appointed to the chair of political economy at the Academy of Lausanne, Switzerland. He retired in 1892. He is generally credited with having founded what subsequently became known, under the leadership of the Italian economist and sociologist Vilfredo Pareto, as the Lausanne school of economists.

In a theoretical work that assumes a "regime of perfectly free competition," Walras constructed a mathematical model in which productive factors, products, and prices automatically adjust in equilibrium. In doing so, he tied together the theories of production, exchange, money, and capital. Walras also advocated the abolition of taxes and the nationalization of private land to generate revenue for the government.

CHAPTER FIVE

WILLIAM STANLEY JEVONS

(b. September 1, 1835, Liverpool, England—
d. August 13, 1882, near Hastings, Sussex)

William Stanley Jevons was an English logician and economist whose book *The Theory of Political Economy* (1871) expounded the "final" (marginal) utility theory of value. Jevons's work, along with similar discoveries made by Carl Menger in Vienna (1871) and by Léon Walras in Switzerland (1874), marked the opening of a new period in the history of economic thought.

Jevons broke off his studies of the natural sciences at University College, London, in 1854 to take a post as assayer in Sydney, Australia. There he became interested in political economy and social studies. After his return to England in 1859, he completed two of his most original and seminal papers. The first, "General Mathematical Theory of Political Economy" (1862), outlined what came to be known as the marginal utility theory of value. This theory suggests that the utility or value to a consumer of an additional unit of a product is (at least beyond some critical quantity) inversely related to the number of units of that product he already owns. The second, "A Serious Fall in the Value of Gold" (1863), attempted to measure the rise in prices in the period following the gold discoveries in California and Australia. This work represents one of the greatest contributions to the theory of index numbers ever published. Yet it was not until the publication of *The Coal Question* (1865), in which Jevons called attention to the gradual exhaustion of Britain's coal supplies, that he received public recognition. He feared that as the supply of coal was exhausted, its price would rise. That conclusion was wrong, however, because it failed to account for improvements in the technology used to extract coal.

In 1866 Jevons was appointed to a chair of political economy at Owens College, Manchester. He moved to University College in 1876. Of his works on logic and scientific method, the most important is his *Principles of Science* (1874). His other notable works include *The Theory of Political Economy* (1871) and *The State in Relation to Labour* (1882).

William Stanley Jevons, engraving. BBC Hulton Picture Library—Globe Photos

CHAPTER SIX

CARL MENGER

(b. February 23, 1840, Neu-Sandec, Galicia, Austrian Empire [now in Poland]—d. February 26, 1921, Vienna, Austria)

The Austrian economist Carl Menger contributed to the development of the marginal utility theory and to the formulation of a subjective theory of value.

Menger received a Ph.D. from the Jagiellonian University in Kraków in 1867 and then accepted a position in the Austrian civil service. In 1873 he became a professor of political economy at the University of Vienna, remaining there, with brief interruptions, until 1903. He then devoted himself to his studies in economics. Menger is widely known as the founder of the Austrian school of economics.

What made Menger (along with economists William Stanley Jevons and Léon Walras) a founder of the marginal utility revolution was the insight that goods are valuable because they serve various uses whose importance differs. Menger used this insight to resolve the diamond-water paradox that Adam Smith posed but never solved. Menger also used it to refute the view, popularized by David Ricardo and Karl Marx, that the value of goods derives from the value of labour used to produce them. Menger proved just the opposite: that the value of labour derives from the value of the goods it produces, which is why, for example, the best professional basketball players or the most popular actors are paid so much.

Menger also used the subjective theory of value to disprove the Aristotelian view that exchange involves a transaction of equal value for equal value. In exchange, Menger pointed out, people will give up what they value less in return for what they value more, which is why both sides can gain from an exchange. That led him to the conclusion that middlemen create value by facilitating exchange. Menger also showed that money, as a transactional medium, solves the difficulty of exchanging goods directly: a chicken farmer who wants gasoline finds it easier to trade those chickens for some widely accepted good—money—and then to trade this good for gasoline. It is far more difficult to trade chickens directly for gasoline. Money, like language, developed naturally as a means for facilitating human interaction.

Menger, detail of a drawing by F. Schmutzer, 1910. Bildarchiv Preussischer Kulturbesitz, Berlin

CHAPTER SEVEN

Alfred Marshall

(b. July 26, 1842, London, England—
d. July 13, 1924, Cambridge, Cambridgeshire)

Alfred Marshall was one of the chief founders of the school of English neoclassical economics and the first principal of University College, Bristol (1877–81).

Marshall was educated at Merchant Taylors' School and at St. John's College, Cambridge. He was a fellow and lecturer in political economy at Balliol College, Oxford, from 1883 to 1885 and a professor of political economy at the University of Cambridge from 1885 to 1908 and thereafter devoted himself to his writing. From 1891 to 1894 he was a member of the Royal Commission on Labour.

Marshall's *Principles of Economics* (1890) was his most important contribution to economic literature. It was distinguished by the introduction of a number of new concepts, such as elasticity of demand, consumer's surplus, quasirent, and the representative firm—all of which played a major role in the subsequent development of economics. In this work Marshall emphasized that the price and output of a good are determined by supply and demand, which act like "blades of the scissors" in determining price. This concept has endured: modern economists trying to understand changes in the price of a particular good start by looking for factors that may have shifted the demand or supply curves.

Marshall's *Industry and Trade* (1919) studied industrial organization; *Money, Credit and Commerce* (1923) was written at a time when the economic world was deeply divided on the theory of value. Marshall succeeded, largely by introducing the element of time as a factor in analysis, in reconciling the classical cost-of-production principle with the marginal utility principle formulated by William Jevons and the Austrian school of economics. Marshall is often considered to have been in the line of notable English economists that includes Adam Smith, David Ricardo, and John Stuart Mill.

CHAPTER EIGHT

EUGEN VON BÖHM-BAWERK

(b. February 12, 1851, Brünn, Moravia, Austrian Empire [now Brno, Czech Republic]—d. August 27, 1914, Kramsach, Tirol, Austria-Hungary [now in Austria])

The Austrian economist and statesman Eugen von Böhm-Bawerk was a leading theorist of the Austrian school of economics.

After graduating from the University of Vienna, Böhm-Bawerk worked in the Austrian Ministry of Finance (1872–75) and was allowed by the ministry to study at several German universities. In 1880 he moved to Innsbruck, and he became a full professor at the university there in 1884. In 1890 he returned to the Ministry of Finance and took part in the currency reform of 1892 and the adoption of the gold standard. He held several cabinet offices in succeeding years before resigning in 1904 to become a professor of economics at the University of Vienna.

Böhm-Bawerk was, with Carl Menger and Friedrich von Wieser, one of the three pillars of the Austrian school of economics. Starting from Menger's work, Böhm-Bawerk developed a theory of the origin and determination of the rate of interest and the period of turnover of capital occurring with the attainment of the market clearing wage. This became the basis of the Austrian school's theory of capital. Through its influence on later writers such as Knut Wicksell and Irving Fisher, this theory provided the basis for the modern treatment of interest, which is now seen as stemming from the interaction of (a) the preference for present goods (which inhibits savings and investment) and (b) the productivity of longer periods of turnover of capital (which causes investment funds to be demanded).

Böhm-Bawerk was the first economist to refute Karl Marx's view that workers are systematically exploited. While Marx attributed productivity to labour, Böhm-Bawerk attributed productivity to an indirect, or "roundabout," process based on an investment in land and labour.

CHAPTER NINE

FRIEDRICH VON WIESER

(b. July 10, 1851, Vienna, Austria—
d. July 23, 1926, Sankt Gilgen)

Friedrich von Wieser was one of the principal members of the Austrian school of economics, along with Carl Menger and Eugen von Böhm-Bawerk.

Wieser attended the University of Vienna from 1868 to 1872 and then entered government service. Like his colleague Böhm-Bawerk, Wieser was permitted to study under the three founders of the German school of historical economics—Karl Knies at Heidelberg, Wilhelm Georg Roscher at Leipzig, and Bruno Hildebrand at Jena. Carl Menger's work exercised a profound influence upon Wieser. In 1884 he went to the University of Prague and in 1903 succeeded Menger at the University of Vienna. He subsequently occupied official positions and served as minister of commerce in the last government of the Austro-Hungarian Empire.

His two most important works are *Der natürliche Wert* (1889; "Natural Value") and *Grundriss der Sozialökonomik* (1914; "Foundations of Social Economy"). In the first of these he developed the Austrian-school theory of costs, building on Menger's subjective-value approach and introducing the concept of opportunity cost. In *Sozialökonomik* the principle of marginal utility is the starting point for an analysis of successively more elaborate systems of economic relationships.

CHAPTER TEN

KNUT WICKSELL

(b. December 20, 1851, Stockholm, Sweden—
d. May 3, 1926, Stocksund)

The Swedish economist Knut Wicksell was internationally renowned for his pioneering work in monetary theory.

In *Geldzins und Güterpreise* (1898; *Interest and Prices*, 1936) he propounded an explanation of price-level movements by an aggregate demand-supply analysis focused on the relations between prospective profit and interest rates. This made Wicksell a forerunner of modern monetary theory and anticipated the work of John Maynard Keynes in *A Treatise on Money* (1930). In *Über Wert, Kapital und Rente* (1893; *Value, Capital and Rent*, 1954), Wicksell emerged as an originator of the marginal productivity theory. There and in other studies he also made striking advances in capital theory.

… CHAPTER ELEVEN

Thorstein Veblen

(b. July 30, 1857, Manitowoc county, Wisconsin, U.S.—d. August 3, 1929, near Menlo Park, California)

Thorstein Veblen was an American economist and social scientist who sought to apply an evolutionary, dynamic approach to the study of economic institutions. With *The Theory of the Leisure Class* (1899) he won fame in literary circles, and, in describing the life of the wealthy, he coined phrases—*conspicuous consumption* and *pecuniary emulation*—that are still widely used.

EARLY LIFE

Veblen was of Norwegian descent. He did not learn English until he went to school, and all of his life he spoke it with an accent. He graduated from Carleton College in Northfield, Minnesota, in three years, proving himself a brilliant scholar and a mocking individualist given to railing at established ideas. He went on to study philosophy at Johns Hopkins and Yale universities, receiving a Ph.D. from Yale in 1884. Unable to find a teaching position, he returned to his father's farm in Minnesota, where he spent most of the next seven years reading. In 1888 he married Ellen Rolfe, a member of a wealthy and influential family. Still unable to find a job, he entered Cornell University in 1891 as a graduate student. There he impressed J. Laurence Laughlin so highly that, when Laughlin was asked to head the economics department at the new University of Chicago in 1892, he took Veblen with him as a fellow in economics. Not until 1896, when Veblen was 39, did he attain the rank of instructor.

His first book, *The Theory of the Leisure Class*, subtitled *An Economic Study of Institutions*, was published in 1899. Still read today, it represents the essence of most of his thinking. Veblen sought to apply Darwin's evolutionism to the study of modern economic life. The industrial system, he wrote, required people to be diligent, efficient, and cooperative, while those who ruled the business world were concerned with making money and displaying their wealth; their outlook was survivalist, a remnant of a predatory, barbarian past. Veblen examined with obvious relish the "modern survivals of prowess" in the amusements, fashions, sports, religion, and aesthetic tastes of the ruling class. The book caught the interest of the literary world, where it was read as satire rather than as science and thereby earned Veblen a reputation as a social critic that extended far beyond his academic horizon.

His reputation, however, did not bring him academic success. He was an indifferent teacher with only contempt for the university ritual of lecture and examination. In 1904 he published *The Theory of Business Enterprise*, in which he expanded on his evolutionary theme of the incompatibility between the modern industrial process and the irrational means of business and finance (i.e., on the difference between making goods and making money).

At Chicago Veblen attained only the rank of assistant professor, and he was forced to leave after being charged with marital infidelity. He was appointed to an associate professorship at Stanford University in 1906. After three years his personal affairs once more became an issue, and he was forced to resign again.

LATER WORKS AND CAREER

With some difficulty Veblen found a post as a lecturer at the University of Missouri, at a much lower salary, and he remained there from 1911 until 1918. He was divorced by Ellen Rolfe and in 1914 married Anne Fessenden Bradley, a divorcée whom he had known for some years.

At Missouri Veblen enjoyed a productive period. In *The Instinct of Workmanship and the State of the Industrial Arts* (1914), he elaborated on his idea that business enterprise was in fundamental conflict with the human propensity for useful effort; too much of humankind's energy was wasted through inefficient institutions. In *An Inquiry into the Nature of Peace and the Terms of Its Perpetuation* (1917), Veblen maintained that modern wars were caused mainly by the competitive demands of national business interests and that an enduring peace could be had only at the expense of "the rights of ownership, and of the price system in which these rights take effect."

In the fall of 1918 he joined the editorial staff of *The Dial*, a literary and political magazine in New York, for which he wrote a series of articles later published in book form as *The Vested Interests and the State of the Industrial Arts* (1919). Another series of articles that

TECHNOCRACY

Technocracy is a system of government by technicians who are guided solely by the imperatives of their technology. The concept developed in the United States early in the 20th century as an expression of the Progressive movement and became a subject of considerable public interest in the 1930s during the Great Depression. The origins of the technocracy movement may be traced to Frederick W. Taylor's introduction of the concept of scientific management. Writers such as Henry L. Gannt, Thorstein Veblen, and Howard Scott suggested that businessmen were incapable of reforming their industries in the public interest and that control of industry should thus be given to engineers.

appeared in *The Dial* was later published in the book *The Engineers and the Price System* (1921). In these pieces Veblen developed his ideas for reform of the economic system. He believed that engineers, who had the knowledge to run industry, should take over its direction because they would manage it for efficiency instead of profit. This theme was central to the brief Depression-era movement known as "technocracy."

FINAL YEARS AND ASSESSMENT

Veblen left *The Dial* after one year. His second wife had suffered a nervous collapse that was followed by her death in 1920. Veblen himself largely had to be looked after by a few devoted friends and appeared to be psychologically incapable of conversing with strangers interested in his ideas. For a while he lectured at the New School for Social Research in New York City, his salary supported by a subsidy from a former student. His last book, *Absentee Ownership and Business Enterprise in Recent Times: The Case of America* (1923), was an ill-written and repetitious examination of corporate finance, in which he stressed again the contradiction between the industrial arts and business enterprise.

In 1926 he gave up teaching and returned to California, where he lived with a stepdaughter in a cabin in the mountains overlooking the sea. He remained there until the end of his life.

Chapter Twelve

John Rogers Commons

(b. October 13, 1862, Hollandsburg, Ohio, U.S.—d. May 11, 1945, Fort Lauderdale, Florida)

John Rogers Commons was an American economist who became the foremost authority on U.S. labour in the first third of the 20th century.

Commons studied at Oberlin College and at Johns Hopkins University and taught at the University of Wisconsin (1904–32). He established his reputation with the publication of *A Documentary History of American Industrial Society*, 10 vol. (1910–11), and *History of Labour in the United States*, 4 vol. (1918–35). Commons's theory of the evolution of the American labour movement in terms of changes in market structure was generally accepted. After World War I, Commons broadened his reputation with the publication of *Legal Foundations of Capitalism* (1924) and its sequel, *Institutional Economics* (1934).

Commons drafted much of the reform legislation that made Wisconsin an example for other states. Such legislation introduced legal privileges for labour unions,

John R. Commons. U.S. Department of Labor

compulsory unemployment insurance, compulsory workers' compensation, and government regulation of utilities. He also made notable contributions to the federal government in the areas of civil service, public utilities, and unemployment insurance and contributed to the design of the Social Security Act of 1935, the U.S. government's first comprehensive program to fund old-age benefits through payroll taxes.

CHAPTER THIRTEEN

WESLEY CLAIR MITCHELL

(b. August 5, 1874, Rushville, Illinois, U.S.—d. October 29, 1948, New York, N.Y.)

The American economist Wesley Clair Mitchell was the world's foremost authority of his day on business cycles.

Mitchell was educated at the University of Chicago, where he came under the influence of Thorstein Veblen and John Dewey. He taught at numerous universities, including the University of Chicago (1900–02), the University of California (1902–12), Columbia University (1913–19; 1922–44), and the New School for Social Research, New York City (1919–21). Despite his extensive teaching, Mitchell was primarily devoted to economic research.

In 1920 he helped to organize the National Bureau of Economic Research and was its director of research until 1945. He served as chief of the price section of the War Industries Board during World War I, as chairman of Pres. Herbert Hoover's Research Committee on Social Trends, and as a member of the National Planning Board (1933) and of the National Resources Board (1934–35).

Wesley C. Mitchell. Courtesy of Columbia University, New York

Under Mitchell's leadership, the Social Science Research Council, of which he was chairman (1927–30), and the Bureau of Educational Experiments greatly influenced the development of quantitative studies of economic behaviour in the United States and abroad.

CHAPTER FOURTEEN

ARTHUR CECIL PIGOU

(b. November 18, 1877, Ryde, Isle of Wight, England—d. March 7, 1959, Cambridge, Cambridgeshire)

Arthur Cecil Pigou was a British economist noted for his studies in welfare economics.

Educated at King's College, Cambridge, Pigou was considered one of Alfred Marshall's best students. When Marshall retired as a professor of political economy in 1908, Pigou was named as Marshall's replacement. Pigou was responsible for disseminating many of Marshall's ideas and thereby provided the leading theoretical basis for what came to be known as the Cambridge school of economics.

In his most influential work, *The Economics of Welfare* (1920), Pigou developed Marshall's concept of externalities, which are the costs imposed or benefits conferred on others that are not accounted for by the person who creates these costs or benefits. Pigou argued that negative externalities (costs imposed) should be offset by a tax, while positive externalities should be offset by a subsidy. Pigou's analysis was widely accepted until the early 1960s, when Ronald Coase showed that taxes and subsidies are not necessary if the partners in the transaction—that is, the people affected by the externality and the people who cause it—can bargain over the transaction. Pigou's reliance on taxes and subsidies was further undercut by public choice economists who observed that governments can and do fail, sometimes more spectacularly than markets.

Pigou applied his economic analysis to a number of other problems, including tariff policy, unemployment, and public finance. He also served on the Royal Commission on Income Tax (1919–20) and on two committees on the currency (1918–19; 1924–25).

CHAPTER FIFTEEN

John Maynard Keynes

(b. June 5, 1883, Cambridge, Cambridgeshire, England—d. April 21, 1946, Firle, Sussex)

The English economist, journalist, and financier John Maynard Keynes is best known for his economic theories (Keynesian economics) on the causes of prolonged unemployment. His most important work, *The General Theory of Employment, Interest and Money* (1935–36), advocated a remedy for economic recession based on a government-sponsored policy of full employment.

BACKGROUND AND EARLY CAREER

Keynes was born into a moderately prosperous family. His father, John Neville Keynes, was an economist and later an academic administrator at King's College, Cambridge. His mother was one of the first female graduates of the same university, which Keynes entered in 1902.

John Maynard Keynes, detail of a watercolour by Gwen Raverat, about 1908; in the National Portrait Gallery, London. Courtesy of the National Portrait Gallery, London

At Cambridge he was influenced by economist Alfred Marshall, who prompted Keynes to shift his academic interests from mathematics and the classics to politics and economics. Cambridge also introduced Keynes to an important group of writers and artists. The early history of the Bloomsbury group—an exclusive circle of the cultural elect, which counted among its members Leonard and Virginia Woolf, the painter Duncan Grant, and the art critic Clive Bell—centred upon Cambridge and the remarkable figure of Lytton Strachey. Strachey, who had entered Cambridge two years before Keynes, inducted the younger man into the exclusive private club known simply as "the Society," whose members and associates were the leading spirits of Bloomsbury.

After earning a B.A. in 1905 and an M.A. in 1909, Keynes became a civil servant, taking a job with the India Office in Whitehall. His experience there formed the basis of his first major work, *Indian Currency and Finance* (1913), a definitive examination of pre-World War I Indian finance and currency. He then returned to Cambridge, where he taught economics until 1915. With the onset of World War I, Keynes returned to government employment, this time in the Treasury.

His performance may have marked Keynes for a public career, but the Versailles Peace Conference changed his aspirations. Accompanying Prime Minister David Lloyd George to France as an economic adviser, Keynes was troubled by the political chicanery and burdensome policies that were to be imposed upon the defeated Germany. He resigned his post, depressed, to quote from a letter to his father, by the impending "devastation of Europe."

In two summer months he composed the indictment of the Versailles settlement that reached the bookstores

John Maynard Keynes. Alfred Eisenstaedt/Time & Life Pictures/Getty Images

by Christmas 1919 as *The Economic Consequences of the Peace*. The permanent importance of this polemical essay lies in its economic analysis of the stringent reparations placed upon Germany and the corresponding lack of probability that the debts would ever be paid. The popular success of the book, however, came from the blistering sketches of Woodrow Wilson, Georges Clemenceau, and Keynes's old chief, Lloyd George.

KEY CONTRIBUTIONS

Keynes was esteemed at Cambridge as the most brilliant student of Marshall and fellow economist Arthur Cecil Pigou, authors of large, definitive works explaining how competitive markets functioned, how businesses operated, and how individuals spent their incomes. After publication of *The Economic Consequences of the Peace*, Keynes resigned his lecture post but stayed on as a fellow of King's College, dividing his time between Cambridge and London.

Although the tone of Keynes's major writings in the 1920s was occasionally skeptical, he did not directly challenge the conventional wisdom of the period that favoured laissez-faire—only slightly tempered by public policy—as the best of all possible social arrangements. It was only later, in *The General Theory of Employment, Interest and Money*, that Keynes provided an economic basis for government jobs programs as a solution to high unemployment. The *General Theory*, as it has come to be called, is one of the most influential economics books in history, yet its lack of clarity still causes economists to debate "what Keynes was really saying." He appeared to suggest that a reduction in wage rates would not reduce unemployment; instead, the key to reducing

DEFICIT FINANCING

In the practice of deficit financing, a government spends more money than it receives as revenue, the difference being made up by borrowing or minting new funds. Although budget deficits may occur for numerous reasons, the term usually refers to a conscious attempt to stimulate the economy by lowering tax rates or increasing government expenditures. The influence of government deficits upon a national economy may be very great. It is widely believed that a budget balanced over the span of a business cycle should replace the old ideal of an annually balanced budget. Some economists have abandoned the balanced budget concept entirely, considering it inadequate as a criterion of public policy.

Deficit financing, however, may also result from government inefficiency, reflecting widespread tax evasion or wasteful spending rather than the operation of a planned countercyclical policy.

unemployment was to increase government spending and to run a budget deficit. Governments, many of them looking for excuses to increase spending, wholeheartedly adopted Keynes's recommendations. Most of his professional colleagues also accepted his views.

LATER WORKS

The *General Theory* was Keynes's last major written work. In 1937 he suffered a severe heart attack. Two years later, though not completely recovered, he returned to teaching at Cambridge, wrote three influential articles on war finance entitled *How to Pay for the War* (1940; later reprinted as *Collected Writings*, vol. 9, 1972), and served once more in the Treasury as an all-purpose adviser. He also played a prominent role at the Bretton Woods Conference in 1944. But the institutions that resulted from that conference, the International Monetary Fund and the World Bank, were more representative of the theories of the United States Treasury than of Keynes's thinking.

His last major public service was his negotiation in the autumn and early winter of 1945 of a multibillion-dollar loan granted by the United States to Britain. Keynes died the following year.

John Maynard Keynes (right) *and Assistant Secretary of the U.S. Treasury Harry Dexter White, 1946.* International Monetary Fund

CHAPTER SIXTEEN

Ragnar Frisch

(b. March 1895, Oslo, Norway—d. January 31, 1973, Oslo)

Ragnar Frisch, a Norwegian econometrician and economist, was a joint winner (with Jan Tinbergen) of the 1969 Nobel Prize in Economic Sciences.

Frisch was educated at the University of Oslo (Ph.D., 1926), where he was appointed to a specially created professorship in 1931, a post he held until his retirement in 1965. He was a pioneer of econometrics—the application of mathematical models and statistical techniques to economic data—and coined this and many other economics terms. One of the founders of the Econometric Society, he also was the editor of *Econometrica* for 21 years. In an article on business cycles, Frisch was likely the first person to have referred to the study of individual firms and industries as "microeconomics." Moreover, he referred to the study of the aggregate economy as "macroeconomics."

Ragnar Frisch. © AP Images

Frisch is particularly famous for the development of large-scale econometric modeling linked to economic planning and national income accounting. Through this type of work, he helped many academically trained economists gain entry into key civil service positions. Frisch was involved with a range of macroeconomic topics, including the trade cycle, production theory, consumer behaviour, and statistical theory. Many of the papers he published are regarded as classics.

CHAPTER SEVENTEEN

Gunnar Myrdal

(b. December 6, 1898, Gustafs, Dalarna, Sweden—d. May 17, 1987, Stockholm)

Gunnar Myrdal was a Swedish economist and sociologist who was awarded the Nobel Prize in Economic Sciences in 1974 (the cowinner was Friedrich A. Hayek). He was regarded as a major theorist of international relations and developmental economics.

Myrdal was educated at Stockholm University, where he earned a law degree in 1923 and a doctorate in economics in 1927. He married Alva Reimer in 1924. After receiving a Rockefeller traveling fellowship in the United States (1929–30), Myrdal became an associate professor at the Institute of International Studies in Geneva (1930–31). He also was professor of political economy (1933–50) and of international economy (1960–67) at Stockholm University; in 1967 he became professor emeritus.

Until the early 1930s Myrdal emphasized pure theory, in sharp contrast to his later concern with applied economics and social problems. In his doctoral dissertation he had examined the role of expectations in price formation, an approach stemming from the work of Frank H. Knight. He applied this theoretical approach to macroeconomics in 1931 when, as a member of the Stockholm school of economics, he delivered the lectures resulting in *Monetary Equilibrium* (1939). These lectures illustrated the distinction between ex ante (or planned) and ex post (or realized) savings and investment.

At the invitation of the Carnegie Corporation, Myrdal explored the social and economic problems of African Americans in 1938–40 and wrote *An American Dilemma: The Negro Problem and Modern Democracy* (1944). In this work Myrdal presented his theory of cumulative causation—that is, of poverty creating poverty. Myrdal also pointed out that two economic policies implemented by Pres. Franklin D. Roosevelt's administration inadvertently destroyed jobs for hundreds of thousands of African Americans. The first such policy involved restrictions on cotton production, instituted to raise the incomes of farm owners. The second policy was the minimum wage, which, Myrdal pointed out, made employers less willing to hire relatively unskilled people, many of whom were African American.

From 1947 to 1957 Myrdal was executive secretary of the United Nations Economic Commission for Europe. In his writings on developmental economics, Myrdal warned that economic development of rich and poor countries might never converge. Instead, the two might possibly diverge, with poor countries locked into producing less-profitable primary goods while rich countries reaped the profits associated with economies of scale.

In other books Myrdal combined his economic research with sociological studies. These include *The Political Element in the Development of Economic Theory* (1930) and *Beyond the Welfare State: Economic Planning and Its International Implications* (1960).

CHAPTER EIGHTEEN

BERTIL OHLIN

(b. April 23, 1899, Klippan, Sweden—
d. August 3, 1979, Vålädalen)

The Swedish economist and political leader Bertil Ohlin is remembered as the founder of the modern theory of the dynamics of trade. In 1977 he shared the Nobel Prize in Economic Sciences with James Meade.

Ohlin studied at the University of Lund and at Stockholm University under Eli Heckscher. He developed an early interest in international trade and presented a thesis on trade theory in 1922. Ohlin studied for a period at both the University of Oxford and Harvard University; at the latter institution he was influenced by Frank Taussig and John H. Williams. He obtained a doctorate from Stockholm University in 1924 and the following year became a professor at the University of Copenhagen. In 1930 he succeeded Heckscher at Stockholm University. At this time Ohlin became engaged in a controversy with John Maynard Keynes, contradicting the latter's view that Germany could not pay war reparations. Ohlin saw reparations as nothing more than large international transfers of buying power. By 1936 Keynes had come around to Ohlin's earlier view. Their debate over reparations contributed to modern theories of unilateral international payments.

In 1933 Ohlin published a work that won him world renown, *Interregional and International Trade*. In it he combined work by Heckscher with approaches formed in his own doctoral thesis. He established a theory of international trade that is now known as the Heckscher-Ohlin theory, which states that if two countries produce two goods and use two factors of production (say, labour and capital) to produce these goods, each will export the good that makes the most use of the factor that is most abundant. The theory also provided the basis for Ohlin's later work on the consequences of protecting real wages. As a member of the Stockholm school of economists, Ohlin also developed, from foundations laid by Knut Wicksell, a theoretical treatment of macroeconomic policy. His work on the importance of aggregate demand anticipated later work by Keynes.

Ohlin served as head of the Liberal Party in Sweden from 1944 to 1967. He was a member of the Riksdag (parliament) from 1938 to 1970 and was minister of commerce (1944–45) in Sweden's wartime government.

CHAPTER NINETEEN

FRIEDRICH AUGUST VON HAYEK

(b. May 8, 1899, Vienna, Austria—
d. March 23, 1992, Freiburg, Germany)

The Austrian-born British economist Friedrich August von Hayek (also known as Friedrich A. Hayek or Friedrich von Hayek) was noted for his criticisms of the Keynesian welfare state and of totalitarian socialism. In 1974 he shared the Nobel Prize in Economic Sciences with the Swedish economist Gunnar Myrdal.

Hayek's father, August, was a physician and a professor of botany at the University of Vienna. His mother, Felicitas, was the daughter of Franz von Juraschek, a professor and later a prominent civil servant. During World War I Hayek served in a field artillery battery on the Italian front, and after the war he enrolled at the University of Vienna. Hayek was attracted to both law and psychology in his early university years, but he settled on law for his first degree in 1921. In 1923, his last year at the university, Hayek studied under the Austrian economist Friedrich von Wieser and was awarded a second doctorate in political economy. He also began working at a temporary government office, where he met Ludwig von Mises, a monetary theorist and the author of a book-length critique of socialism.

Von Mises quickly became Hayek's mentor. After a trip to the United States in 1923–24, Hayek returned to Vienna, married, and with von Mises's assistance became the director of the newly founded Austrian Institute for Business Cycle Research. Hayek also became a regular attendee at von Mises's biweekly seminar and published his first book, *Monetary Theory and the Trade Cycle*, in 1929.

In early 1931 Hayek presented four lectures on monetary economics at the London School of Economics and Political Science (LSE). The lectures would ultimately lead to his appointment the following year as the Tooke Professor of Economic Science and Statistics at LSE, where Hayek remained until 1950, having become a naturalized British subject in 1938. Immediately upon arriving in England, Hayek became embroiled in a debate with University of Cambridge economist John Maynard Keynes over their respective theories about the role and effect of money within a developed economy. Both economists were criticized by other economists, and this caused each to rethink his framework. Keynes finished first, publishing in 1936 what would become perhaps the most famous economics book of the century, *The General Theory of Employment, Interest and Money*. Hayek's own book, *The Pure Theory of Capital*, did not appear until 1941, and both World War II and the book's opaqueness caused it to be much less noticed than Keynes's work.

In the mid-1930s Hayek also participated in a debate among economists on the merits of socialism. Those discussions would help shape his later ideas on economics and knowledge, eventually presented in his 1936 presidential address to the London Economic Club. During the war years LSE evacuated to Cambridge. There Hayek worked on his Abuse of Reason project, a wide-ranging critique of an assortment of doctrines that he lumped

WELFARE STATE

A welfare state is a state in which the government plays a key role in the protection and promotion of the economic and social well-being of citizens. The notion of the welfare state is based on the principles of equality of opportunity, equitable distribution of wealth, and public responsibility for those unable to avail themselves of the minimal provisions for a good life. The general term may cover a variety of forms of economic and social organization.

A fundamental feature of the welfare state is social insurance, a provision common to most advanced industrialized countries (e.g., National Insurance in the United Kingdom and Social Security in the United States). Such insurance is usually financed by compulsory contributions and is intended to provide benefits to persons and families during periods of greatest need. It is widely recognized, however, that in practice these cash benefits fall considerably short of the levels intended by the designers of the plans.

The welfare state also usually includes public provision of basic education, health services, and housing (in some cases at low cost or without charge). In these respects the welfare state is considerably more extensive in western European countries than in the United States, featuring in many cases comprehensive health coverage and provision of state-subsidized tertiary education.

Antipoverty programs and the system of personal taxation may also be regarded as aspects of the welfare state. Personal taxation falls into this category insofar as its progressivity is used to achieve greater justice in income distribution (rather than merely to raise revenue) and also insofar as it is used to finance social insurance payments and other benefits not completely financed by compulsory contributions.

together under the label of "scientism," which he defined as "the slavish imitation of the method and language of Science" by social scientists who had appropriated the methods of the natural sciences in areas where they did not apply. Although the project as originally envisioned was never completed, it became the basis for a number of essays and also led to the 1944 publication of Hayek's most famous book, *The Road to Serfdom*, in which he argued that state intervention in the economy aimed at the redistribution of wealth leads inevitably to totalitarianism. In the same year Hayek was elected as a fellow of the British Academy.

In 1950 Hayek left LSE for a position on the newly formed Committee on Social Thought at the University of Chicago. In 1952 his book on psychology, *The Sensory Order*, was published, as was a collection of his essays from the Abuse of Reason project under the title *The Counter-Revolution of Science: Studies on the Abuse of Reason*. Hayek would spend 12 years at Chicago. While there he wrote articles on a number of themes, among them political philosophy, the history of ideas, and social-science methodology. Aspects of his wide-ranging research were woven into his 1960 book on political philosophy, *The Constitution of Liberty*.

In 1962 Hayek left Chicago for the University of Freiburg im Breisgau in West Germany. He remained there until his retirement in 1968, when he accepted an honorary professorship at the University of Salzburg in Austria. In 1974 Hayek was awarded the Nobel Prize in Economic Sciences, which, ironically, he shared with Gunnar Myrdal, whose political and economic views were often opposed to his.

Hayek returned to Freiburg permanently in 1977 and finished work on what would become the three-part *Law,*

Legislation and Liberty (1973–79), a critique of efforts to redistribute incomes in the name of social justice. Later in the 1970s Hayek's monograph *The Denationalization of Money* was published by the Institute of Economic Affairs in London, one of the many classical liberal think tanks that Hayek, directly or indirectly, had a hand in establishing.

In the early 1980s Hayek began writing what would be his final book, a critique of socialism. Because his health was deteriorating, another scholar, philosopher William W. Bartley III, helped edit the ultimate volume, *The Fatal Conceit*, which was published in 1988.

CHAPTER TWENTY

EDWARD HASTINGS CHAMBERLIN

(b. May 18, 1899, La Conner, Washington, U.S.—
d. July 16, 1967, Cambridge, Massachusetts)

Edward Hastings Chamberlin was an American economist known for his theories on industrial monopolies and competition.

Chamberlin studied at the University of Iowa, where he was influenced by the economist Frank H. Knight. He pursued graduate work at the University of Michigan and in 1927 obtained a Ph.D. from Harvard University, where he stayed for the rest of his academic career. His doctoral thesis became the basis for *Theory of Monopolistic Competition* (1933), a book that spurred discussion of competition, especially between firms whose consumers have preferences for particular products and firms that control the prices of their products without being monopolists.

The solutions that Chamberlin proposed are similar to those put forth by British economist Joan Robinson at the University of Cambridge, whose book was published a few months after Chamberlin's. Chamberlin's work offers the deepest insight into the workings of an economy in which firms actively compete by advertising, seeking locational advantage, and differentiating their products. Indeed, Chamberlin is the economist who coined the term *product differentiation*.

One of the implications of Chamberlin's model is that firms in a monopolistically competitive industry will be "too small" relative to their size if they do not differentiate their products. Chamberlin himself, however, considered small size a necessity if consumers are to have the variety they desire.

CHAPTER TWENTY-ONE

Sir Roy Harrod

(b. February 13, 1900, London—d. March 9, 1978, Holt, Norfolk, England)

Sir Roy Harrod was a British economist who pioneered the economics of dynamic growth and the field of macroeconomics.

Harrod was educated at Oxford and at Cambridge, where he was a student of John Maynard Keynes. His career at Christ Church, Oxford (1922–67), was interrupted by World War II service (1940–42) under Frederick Lindemann (later Lord Cherwell) as adviser to Winston Churchill. He was also an adviser to the International Monetary Fund (1952–53). He was knighted in 1959.

Harrod first formulated his concepts of growth dynamics in the 1930s and '40s, emphasizing the analysis of the determining factors, rather than the quantities, of equilibrium growth rates. These ideas were put forth in (1948). The Harrod-Domar model of economic growth (named for Harrod and the U.S. economist E.D. Domar) has been applied to the problems of economic development.

Harrod also wrote *International Economics* (1933), *The Trade Cycle* (1936), *Economic Essays* (1952), *The International Monetary Fund* (1966), *Towards a New Economic Policy* (1967), and *Economic Dynamics* (1973); as a biographer he wrote *The Life of John Maynard Keynes* (1951) and *The Prof: A Personal Memoir of Lord Cherwell* (1959).

CHAPTER TWENTY-TWO

SIMON KUZNETS

(b. April 30 [April 17, Old Style], 1901, Kharkov, Ukraine, Russian Empire [now Kharkiv, Ukraine]—d. July 8, 1985, Cambridge, Massachusetts, U.S.)

Simon Kuznets was a Russian-born American economist and statistician who won the 1971 Nobel Prize in Economic Sciences.

Kuznets immigrated to the United States in 1922, 15 years after the arrival there of his father (who changed the family name to Smith, though the young Kuznets preferred the original name). He was educated at Columbia University, receiving a Ph.D. in 1926. In 1927 he joined the National Bureau of Economic Research, working with its founder, Wesley Mitchell. It was there that Kuznets developed his pioneering studies of U.S. national income and his more general work on economic time series, resulting in comprehensive studies of the economic growth of nations. His study of American national income began with statistics from 1869, encompassing a long-term approach that had never been attempted. Out of this work came an understanding of how to measure gross national product (GNP). Kuznets's research set high standards for all similar studies that would follow. After his work with the federal government, Kuznets taught at the University of Pennsylvania (1930–54), Johns Hopkins University (1954–60), and Harvard University (1960–71).

In all his research, Kuznets emphasized the complexity of fundamental economic data by stressing that reliable results can be derived only through large numbers of observations. Likewise, he criticized the limitations inherent in simple economic models based, for example, on one phase of historical experience. Kuznets insisted that economic data must include information on population structure, technology, the quality of labour, government structure, trade, and markets in order to provide an accurate model. He broke convention by emphasizing, on the basis of the statistical series that he accumulated, how little of economic growth could actually be attributed to the accumulation of labour and capital. He also identified cyclic variations in growth rates (now called "Kuznets cycles") and linked them with underlying factors such as population.

Kuznets received the Nobel Prize for empirical work that led him to identify the nexus of modern economic development. According to Kuznets, the epoch of "modern economic growth" began in northwestern Europe in the last half of the 18th century and later spread south and east, reaching Russia and Japan by the end of the 19th century. Through this study Kuznets determined that per capita income rose by 15 percent or more each decade, a rate which had been unheard of in precapitalist societies.

Simon Kuznets. © AP Images

CHAPTER TWENTY-THREE

THEODORE WILLIAM SCHULTZ

(b. April 30, 1902, near Arlington, South Dakota, U.S.—d. February 26, 1998, Evanston, Illinois)

Theodore William Schultz was an American agricultural economist whose influential studies of the role of "human capital"—education, talent, energy, and will—in economic development won him a share (with Sir Arthur Lewis) of the 1979 Nobel Prize in Economic Sciences.

Schultz graduated from South Dakota State College in 1927 and earned a Ph.D. in 1930 at the University of Wisconsin, where he was influenced by John R. Commons and other reform-minded thinkers. He taught at Iowa State College (1930–43) and at the University of Chicago (1943–1972), where he was head of the economics department from 1946 to 1961.

In *Transforming Traditional Agriculture* (1964), Schultz challenged the prevailing view, held by development economists, that farmers in developing countries were irrational in their unwillingness to innovate. He argued that, to the contrary, the farmers were making rational responses to high taxes and artificially low crop prices set by their governments. Schultz also noted that governments in developing countries lacked the agricultural extension services critical for training farmers in new methods. He viewed agricultural development as a precondition for industrialization.

As an empirical economist, Schultz visited farms when he traveled to gain a better understanding of agricultural economics. After World War II, he met an elderly and apparently poor farm couple who seemed quite content with their life. He asked them why. They answered that they were not poor; earnings from their farm had allowed them to send four children to college, and they believed that education would enhance their children's productivity and, consequently, their income. That conversation led Schultz to formulate his concept of human capital, which he concluded could be studied by using the same terms applied to nonhuman capital. Human capital, however, could be expressed in the form of productive knowledge.

CHAPTER TWENTY-FOUR

JAN TINBERGEN

(b. April 12, 1903, The Hague, Netherlands—
d. June 9, 1994, Netherlands)

The Dutch economist Jan Tinbergen was noted for his development of econometric models. He was the cowinner (with Ragnar Frisch) of the first Nobel Prize in Economic Sciences, in 1969.

Tinbergen was the brother of the zoologist Nikolaas Tinbergen and was educated at the University of Leiden. He served as a business-cycle statistician with the Dutch government's Central Bureau of Statistics (1929–36, 1938–45) before becoming the director of the Central Planning Bureau (1945–55). From 1933 to 1973 he was also a professor of economics at the Netherlands School of Economics (now part of Erasmus University), Rotterdam, and he then taught for two years at the University of Leiden before retiring in 1975.

While acting as an economic adviser to the League of Nations at Geneva (1936–38), Tinbergen analyzed economic development in the United States from 1919 to 1932. This pioneering econometric study offered a foundation for his business-cycle theory and guidelines for economic stabilization. He also constructed an econometric model that helped shape both short-term and broader political-economic planning in the Netherlands.

Because of the political nature of his economic analyses, Tinbergen was one of the first to show that a government with multiple policy objectives, such as full employment and price stability, must be able to draw on multiple economic policy tools—say, monetary policy and fiscal policy—to achieve the desired results. Among his major works are *Statistical Testing of Business Cycles* (1938), *Econometrics* (1942), *Economic Policy* (1956), and *Income Distribution* (1975).

Jan Tinbergen. AFP/Getty Images

Chapter Twenty-Five

Sir John Richard Hicks

(b. April 8, 1904, Leamington Spa, Warwickshire, England—d. May 20, 1989, Blockley, Gloucestershire)

Sir John Richard Hicks was an English economist who made pioneering contributions to general economic equilibrium theory and, in 1972, shared (with Kenneth Joseph Arrow) the Nobel Prize in Economic Sciences. He was knighted in 1964.

Although Hicks made major contributions to many areas of 20th-century economics, four in particular stand out. First, he showed that, contrary to what Karl Marx had believed, labour-saving technological progress does not necessarily reduce labour's share of the income. Second, he devised a diagram—the IS-LM diagram—that graphically depicts John M. Keynes's conclusion that an economy can be in equilibrium with less-than-full employment. Third, through his book *Value and Capital* (1939), Hicks showed that much of what economists believe about value theory (the theory about why goods have value) can be reached without the assumption that utility is measurable. Fourth, he came up with a way to judge the impact of changes in government policy. He proposed a compensation test that could compare the losses for the losers with the gains for the winners. If those who gain could, in principle, compensate those who lose—even if they do not actually and directly compensate them—then, claimed Hicks, the change in policy would be efficient.

# CHAPTER TWENTY-SIX

WASSILY LEONTIEF

(b. August 5, 1906, St. Petersburg, Russia—d. February 5, 1999, New York, New York, U.S.)

The Russian-born American economist Wassily Leontief has been called the father of input-output analysis in econometrics. He won the Nobel Prize for Economics in 1973.

Leontief was a student at the University of Leningrad (1921–25) and the University of Berlin (1925–28). He immigrated to the United States in 1931, teaching at Harvard University from 1931 to 1975. From 1948 to 1975 he was director of the Harvard Economic Research Project on the Structure of the American Economy. From 1975 until his death he was a professor of economics at New York University; he was named director of the school's Institute for Economic Analysis in 1978.

The core of his complex input-output system is a gridlike table showing what individual industries buy from and sell to one another. With the addition of government, consumers, foreign countries, and other elements, there emerges a general outline of the goods and services circulating in a national economy. The input-output method of economic analysis is used in various forms by a large number of industrialized countries for both planning and forecasting.

Leontief is also distinguished for having developed linear programming, a mathematical technique for solving complex problems of economic operations. He also is known for the "Leontief Paradox." Economists had previously held that a country's exports reflect the commodity most abundant in that country—i.e., labour or capital. However, as Leontief pointed out, though the United States has more capital than most other nations, the majority of its exports were of labour-intensive goods; conversely, the majority of U.S. imports were of capital-intensive goods. This phenomenon came to be known as the Leontief Paradox.

CHAPTER TWENTY-SEVEN

JAMES EDWARD MEADE

(b. June 23, 1907, Swanage, Dorset, England—d. December 22, 1995, Cambridge, Cambridgeshire)

James Edward Meade was a British economist whose work on international economic policy procured him (with Bertil Ohlin) the Nobel Prize in Economic Sciences in 1977.

Meade was educated at Malvern College and at Oriel College, Oxford, where he earned first-class honours in 1928. In 1930–31 he spent a postgraduate year at Trinity College, Cambridge, where he became involved in discussions of John Maynard Keynes's *Treatise on Money* that led to the development of Keynes's *General Theory of Employment, Interest, and Money* (1936). It was perhaps this period that gave Meade's policy work its distinctly Cambridge and somewhat leftist flavour. He served as a war economist during World War II and was the leading economist in the Labour government (1946–47). He held chairs at the London School of Economics (1947–57) and at Cambridge (1957–68).

Meade's early important work resulted in *The Theory of International Economic Policy*, which was published in two volumes—*The Balance of Payments* (1951) and *Trade and Welfare* (1955). In the first of these books he sought to synthesize Keynesian and neoclassical elements in a model designed to show the effects of various monetary and fiscal policies on the balance of payments. In the second volume Meade explored the effects on economic welfare of various kinds of trade policy, providing a detailed analysis of the welfare effects of regulation of trade. Meade's work also led to later work on trade discrimination and effective protection.

CHAPTER TWENTY-EIGHT

JOHN KENNETH GALBRAITH

(b. October 15, 1908, Iona Station, Ontario, Canada—d. April 29, 2006, Cambridge, Massachusetts, U.S.)

The Canadian-born American economist and public servant John Kenneth Galbraith was known for his support of public spending and for the literary quality of his writing on public affairs.

After study at the University of Toronto's Ontario Agricultural College (now part of the University of Guelph; B.S., 1931) and the University of California, Berkeley (Ph.D., 1934), Galbraith, who became a U.S. citizen in 1937, taught successively at Harvard and Princeton universities until 1942. During World War II and the postwar period, he held a variety of government posts and served as editor of *Fortune* magazine (1943–48) before resuming his academic career at Harvard in 1948. He established himself as a politically active liberal academician with a talent for communicating with the reading public. A key adviser to Pres. John F. Kennedy, Galbraith served as ambassador to India from 1961 to 1963, when he returned again to Harvard; he became professor emeritus in 1975. He also continued his involvement in public affairs, and in 1967–68 he was national chairman of Americans for Democratic Action.

Galbraith's major works include *American Capitalism: The Concept of Countervailing Power* (1951), in which he questioned the competitive ideal in industrial organization. In his popular critique of the wealth gap, *The Affluent Society* (1958), Galbraith faulted the "conventional wisdom" of American economic policies and called for less spending on consumer goods and more spending on government programs. In *The New Industrial State* (1967) he envisioned a growing similarity between "managerial" capitalism and socialism and called for intellectual and political changes to stem what he saw as a decline of competitiveness in the American economy. He was awarded the Presidential Medal of Freedom in 1946 and 2000.

John Kenneth Galbraith. Diana Walker/Time & Life Pictures/Getty Images

Chapter Twenty-Nine

Tjalling Charles Koopmans

(b. August 28, 1910, Graveland, Netherlands—
d. February 26, 1985, New Haven, Connecticut, U.S.)

Tjalling Charles Koopmans was a Dutch-born American economist who shared—with Leonid Vitalyevich Kantorovich of the Soviet Union—the Nobel Prize in Economic Sciences in 1975. The two men independently developed a rational method, called activity analysis, for allocating resources so as to attain a given economic objective at the lowest cost.

Koopmans was educated in mathematics and physics at the universities of Utrecht and Leiden, obtaining a Ph.D. in economics at Leiden in 1936. In 1940 he went to the United States, where he worked for the British Merchant Shipping Mission during World War II. In that position he was concerned with the selection of shipping routes that would minimize the total cost of transporting required quantities of goods, available at various locations in America, to specified destinations in England. He showed that the desired result is obtainable by the straightforward solution of a system of equations involving the costs of the materials at their sources and the costs of shipping them by alternative routes. He also devised a general mathematical model of the problem that led to the necessary equations.

In 1944 Koopmans joined the Cowles Commission for Research in Economics at the University of Chicago, where he extended his technique to a wide variety of economic problems. When the commission was relocated to Yale University in 1955, Koopmans moved with it, becoming professor of economics at Yale. He wrote a widely read book on the methodology of economic analysis, *Three Essays on the State of Economic Science* (1957). Koopmans became a naturalized U.S. citizen in 1946.

CHAPTER THIRTY

RONALD COASE

(b. December 29, 1910, Willesden, Middlesex, England)

The British-born American economist Ronald Coase was among the originators of the field known as new institutional economics, which attempts to explain political, legal, and social institutions in economic terms and to understand the role of institutions in fostering and impeding economic growth. He was awarded the Nobel Prize in Economic Sciences in 1991.

Coase attended the London School of Economics, where he received a bachelor of commerce degree in 1932 and a Ph.D. in economics in 1951. He was employed at various universities, including the London School of Economics (1935–51), the University of Buffalo, New York (1951–58), the University of Virginia, Charlottesville (1958–64), and the University of Chicago Law School, where he was professor of economics from 1964 and professor emeritus of economics and senior fellow in law and economics from 1982. He was editor of the *Journal of Law and Economics* from 1964 to 1982 and founding president of the International Society for New Institutional Economics from 1996 to 1997. From its creation in 2000 he served as research adviser to the Ronald Coase Institute, which promotes the study of new institutional economics.

Coase did pioneering work on the ways in which transaction costs and property rights affect business and society. In his most famous paper, "The Problem of Social Cost" (1960), he developed what later became known as the Coase theorem. In the paper, Coase argued that nuisances are the product of joint causation and that, when information and transaction costs are low, the market will produce an efficient solution to the problem of nuisances without regard to where the law places the liability for the nuisance. His work was a call to legal scholars to consider the process of bargaining about rights outside the context of litigation. The Royal Swedish Academy of Sciences cited Coase for this research and also for "pioneering the study of how property rights are distributed among individuals by law, contract, and regulations, showing that this determines how economic decisions are made and whether they will succeed."

CHAPTER THIRTY-ONE

GEORGE JOSEPH STIGLER

(b. January 17, 1911, Renton, Washington, U.S.—
d. December 1, 1991, Chicago, Illinois)

The American economist George Joseph Stigler's incisive and unorthodox studies of marketplace behaviour and the effects of government regulation won him the 1982 Nobel Prize in Economic Sciences.

After graduating from the University of Washington in 1931, Stigler took a business degree at Northwestern University in 1932 and a Ph.D. in economics at the University of Chicago in 1938. He taught at Iowa State College in 1936–38, the University of Minnesota in 1938–46, Brown University in 1946–47, Columbia University in 1947–58, and the University of Chicago from 1958. From 1963 he was Charles R. Walgreen distinguished service professor of American institutions, becoming emeritus in 1981. At Chicago he founded in 1977 the Center for the Study of the Economy and the State.

Among Stigler's notable contributions to economics were his study of the economics of information, an important elaboration of the traditional understanding of how efficient markets operate, and his studies of public regulation, in which he concluded that at best it has little influence and that it is usually detrimental to consumer interests.

CHAPTER THIRTY-TWO

Maurice Allais

(b. May 31, 1911, Paris, France—
d. October 9, 2010, Saint-Cloud)

The French economist Maurice Allais was awarded the Nobel Prize in Economic Sciences in 1988 for his development of principles to guide efficient pricing and resource allocation in large monopolistic enterprises.

Allais studied economics at the École Polytechnique (Polytechnic School) and then at the École Nationale Supérieure des Mines de Paris (National School of Mines in Paris). In 1937 he began working for the state-owned French mine administration, and in 1944 he became a professor at the École des Mines. From the mid-1940s on, he directed an economics research unit at the Centre de la Recherche Scientifique (National Centre for Scientific Research).

In his groundbreaking theoretical work, Allais sought to balance social benefits with economic efficiency in the pricing plans of state-owned monopolies such as utility companies. His principles caused state enterprises to consider ways that the pricing of goods or services could achieve results formerly achieved through regulation alone. His work proved particularly important in the decades following World War II, when the state-owned monopolies of western Europe saw tremendous growth.

Allais's work paralleled, and sometimes preceded, similar works by Sir John Hicks and Paul Samuelson.

According to Samuelson, "Had Allais's earliest writings been in English, a generation of economic theory would have taken a different course."

Allais received numerous honours and awards. He was a member of several academies and learned societies, including the Institut de France, the U.S. National Academy of Sciences, the Lincean Academy in Italy, and the Russian Academy of Sciences. In 1977 he was named an officer of the Legion of Honour, the premier order of the French republic; he was made grand officer in 2005.

CHAPTER THIRTY-THREE

TRYGVE HAAVELMO

(b. December 13, 1911, Skedsmo, Norway—
d. July 28, 1999, Norway)

The Norwegian economist Trygve Haavelmo was a pioneer in what became the field of economic forecasting. In 1989 he was awarded the Nobel Prize in Economic Sciences.

After the outbreak of World War II, Haavelmo left Norway and delivered his doctoral dissertation, "The Probability Approach in Econometrics," at Harvard University in 1941. Although he had two doctorates from the University of Oslo, his innovative dissertation, cited by the Nobel committee for its influence, was first published in 1944 in an American periodical, *Econometrica*. During the 1940s Haavelmo taught at the University of Chicago (where he was also a visiting professor in the late 1950s) before returning to Norway in 1947. He retired from the University of Oslo faculty in 1979, becoming professor emeritus.

Haavelmo's statistical techniques made possible the development of econometric models that predict how a change in one aspect of the economy will affect others; that is, he demonstrated that statistical probability theory could be integrated into economic formulations. His econometrics contributed to the techniques of national economic forecasting, allowing a more accurate formulation of government economic policies.

CHAPTER THIRTY-FOUR

LEONID VITALYEVICH KANTOROVICH

(b. January 19 [January 6, Old Style], 1912, St. Petersburg, Russia—d. April 7, 1986, U.S.S.R.)

Leonid Vitalyevich Kantorovich was a Soviet mathematician and economist who shared the 1975 Nobel Prize in Economic Sciences with Tjalling Charles Koopmans for their work on the optimal allocation of scarce resources.

Kantorovich was educated at Leningrad State University and received a doctorate in mathematics (1930) at the age of 18. He became a professor at Leningrad in 1934, a position he held until 1960. He headed the department of mathematics and economics in the Siberian branch of the U.S.S.R. Academy of Sciences from 1961 to 1971 and then served as head of the research laboratory at Moscow's Institute of National Economic Planning (1971–76). Kantorovich was elected to the prestigious Academy of Sciences of the Soviet Union (1964) and was awarded the Lenin Prize in 1965.

His first major contribution to economics came in 1938 as a consultant to the Soviet government's Laboratory of the Plywood Trust. Kantorovich realized that the problem of maximizing the distribution of raw materials could be solved in mathematical terms. The linear technique he developed is now called "linear programming."

Kantorovich was a notable "reform" economist whose nondogmatic critical analyses of Soviet economic policy clashed with the views of his orthodox Marxist colleagues. In a 1939 book, *The Mathematical Method of Production Planning and Organization*, he showed that all problems of economic allocation can be reduced to maximizing a function subject to constraints. At the same time, economists John Hicks (in the United Kingdom) and Paul Samuelson (in the United States) were reaching the same conclusion. In his best-known book, *The Best Use of Economic Resources* (1959), Kantorovich demonstrated that even socialist economies must use prices, based on resource scarcity, to allocate resources efficiently.

CHAPTER THIRTY-FIVE

MILTON FRIEDMAN

(b. July 31, 1912, Brooklyn, New York, U.S.—
d. November 16, 2006, San Francisco, California)

Milton Friedman was an American economist and educator and one of the leading proponents of monetarism in the second half of the 20th century. He was awarded the Nobel Prize in Economic Sciences in 1976.

Friedman won a scholarship to Rutgers University, studied mathematics and economics, and earned a bachelor's degree there in 1932. While at Rutgers he encountered Arthur Burns, then a new assistant professor of economics, whom Friedman ultimately regarded as his mentor and most important influence. Friedman continued his economics studies at the University of Chicago (A.M., 1933) and Columbia University (Ph.D., 1946). In the early years of World War II, he worked at the Department of Treasury in the Division of Tax Research and later for the Statistical Research Group at Columbia University, where he was a member of a team that applied statistical analysis to war research.

In 1946 he accepted a position in the economics department at the University of Chicago, which, except for occasional sabbaticals or visiting appointments, would be his academic home for the next 30 years. He became a full professor in 1948, was named the Paul Snowden Russell Distinguished Service Professor of

MONEY SUPPLY

The term *money supply* refers to the liquid assets held by individuals and banks. It includes coin, currency, and demand deposits (checking accounts). Some economists consider time and savings deposits to be part of the money supply because such deposits can be managed by governmental action and are involved in aggregate economic activity. These deposits are nearly as liquid as currency and demand deposits. Other economists believe that deposits in mutual savings banks, savings and loan associations, and credit unions should be counted as part of the money supply.

The Federal Reserve Board in the United States and the Bank of England in the United Kingdom regulate the money supply to stabilize their respective economies. The Federal Reserve Board, for example, can buy or sell government securities, thereby expanding or contracting the money supply

---

Economics in 1962, and became an emeritus professor in 1983.

At Chicago Friedman taught courses in price theory and monetary economics, and in 1953 he established the Money and Banking Workshop—an important forum for faculty members, graduate students working on dissertations in the field, and occasional outside visitors. The workshop became renowned for the presentation and critical appraisal of papers in monetary economics.

In 1947 Friedman attended the opening meeting of the Mont Pèlerin Society, an organization founded by Friedrich August von Hayek and dedicated to the study and preservation of free societies. Friedman would later say that his participation at the meeting "marked the beginning of my active involvement in the political process." His multifold involvement included advising Presidents Richard M. Nixon and Ronald W. Reagan on economic policy and participating in various institutes and societies.

Friedman's public policy positions included support of flexible exchange rates and a monetary growth rule, the promotion of school vouchers, a balanced budget amendment, and the decriminalization of drugs; he opposed conscription and various forms of price controls—from the minimum wage to rent controls.

Friedman's best-known contributions are in the realm of monetary economics, where he is seen as the

Milton Friedman. George Rose/Getty Images

founder of monetarism and as one of the successors of the "Chicago school" tradition of economics. In the 1950s macroeconomics was dominated by scholars who adhered to theories promoted by John Maynard Keynes. Keynesians believed in using government-sponsored policy to counteract the business cycle, and they held that fiscal policy was more effective than monetary policy in neutralizing, for example, the effects of a recession. Friedman opposed the Keynesian orthodoxy that "money does not matter," instead promoting the view that changes in the money supply affect real economic activity in the short run and the price level in the long run.

In 1976, the year he retired from the University of Chicago, Friedman was awarded the Nobel Prize in Economic Sciences. In 1977 he became a member of the Hoover Institution in Palo Alto, California. About the same time he began work with his wife, Rose, on *Free to Choose*, a book extolling the virtues of a free market system that eventually led to a Public Broadcasting Service (PBS) television series and a set of educational videos of the same name. In 1998 the Friedmans published their memoirs, *Two Lucky People*.

CHAPTER THIRTY-SIX

SIR RICHARD STONE

(b. August 30, 1913, London, England—
d. December 6, 1991, Cambridge, Cambridgeshire)

The British economist Sir Richard Stone received the Nobel Prize in Economic Sciences in 1984 for developing an accounting model that could be used to track economic activities on a national and, later, an international scale. He is sometimes known as the father of national income accounting.

Stone initially studied law at the University of Cambridge, but, under the influence of the economist John Maynard Keynes, he took a degree in economics in 1935 (Sc.D., 1957). He worked for a brokerage firm in London (1936–40), and in 1940, at the invitation of Keynes, he entered the British government's Central Statistical Office. After World War II he was appointed director of the new department of applied economics at Cambridge. He retained that position until 1955, when he became P.D. Leake professor of finance and accounting at Cambridge (1955–80; professor emeritus from 1980). He was knighted in 1978.

The first official estimates of British national income and expenditures were made according to Stone's method in 1941. The greater part of Stone's work, however, was done in the 1950s, when he offered the first concrete statistical means by which to measure investment, government spending, and consumption; these models resulted in what was, in essence, a national bookkeeping system. He went on to adapt his models for such international organizations as the United Nations.

CHAPTER THIRTY-SEVEN

WILLIAM VICKREY

(b. June 21, 1914, Victoria, British Columbia, Canada—d. October 11, 1996, Harrison, New York, U.S.)

William Vickrey was a Canadian-born American economist who brought innovative analysis to the problems of incomplete, or asymmetrical, information. He shared the 1996 Nobel Prize in Economic Sciences with the British economist James Alexander Mirrlees.

Vickrey's family moved from Canada to New York when he was three months old. He was educated at Yale University (B.S., 1935) and Columbia University (M.A., 1937; Ph.D., 1947), where he taught throughout his career. A Quaker, he was a conscientious objector during World War II and spent those years performing public service and developing an inheritance tax for Puerto Rico.

Vickrey had a keen interest in human welfare, often choosing projects with practical applications. His studies of traffic congestion concluded that pricing on commuter trains and toll roads should vary according to usage, with higher fees levied during peak-use periods. This congestion pricing was later adopted by electric and telephone utilities and airlines. In his doctoral thesis, published as *Agenda for Progressive Taxation* (1947), he advocated an "optimal income tax" that would be based on long-term earnings rather than on yearly income.

In awarding him the 1996 Nobel Prize, the selection committee specifically cited his novel approach to auctioneering (now known as a "Vickrey auction"), which, through sealed bidding, awards the auctioned item to the highest bidder but at the price submitted by the second highest bidder. This method, said Vickrey, benefits both buyer and seller by guaranteeing bids that reflect the fair value of the item. Vickrey did not live to receive the Nobel Prize. In the flurry of activity that followed the Nobel announcement, he died of a heart attack just three days after being named.

William Vickrey. © AP Images

CHAPTER THIRTY-EIGHT

Sir Arthur Lewis

(b. January 23, 1915, Castries, Saint Lucia, British West Indies—d. June 15, 1991, Bridgetown, Barbados)

Sir Arthur Lewis was a Saint Lucian economist who shared (with Theodore William Schultz, an American) the 1979 Nobel Prize in Economic Sciences for his studies of economic development and his construction of an innovative model relating the terms of trade between less developed and more developed nations to their respective levels of labour productivity in agriculture.

Lewis attended the London School of Economics after winning a government scholarship. He graduated in 1937 and received a Ph.D. in economics there in 1940. He was a lecturer at the school from 1938 to 1947, professor of economics at the University of Manchester from 1947 to 1958, principal of University College of the West Indies in 1959–62, and professor at Princeton University from 1963 to 1983. He served as adviser on economic development to many international commissions and to several African, Asian, and Caribbean governments. He helped establish, and in 1970–73 headed, the Caribbean Development Bank. Lewis was knighted in 1963.

CHAPTER THIRTY-NINE

PAUL SAMUELSON

(b. May 15, 1915, Gary, Indiana, U.S.—
d. December 13, 2009, Belmont, Massachusetts)

The American economist Paul Samuelson was awarded the Nobel Prize in Economic Sciences in 1970 for his fundamental contributions to nearly all branches of economic theory.

Samuelson was educated at the University of Chicago (B.A., 1935) and at Harvard University (Ph.D., 1941). He became a professor of economics at the Massachusetts Institute of Technology (MIT) in 1940. He also served as an economic adviser to the United States government.

Samuelson contributed to many areas of economic theory through powerful mathematical techniques that he employed essentially as puzzle-solving devices. His *Foundations of Economic Analysis* (1947) provides the basic theme of his work, with the universal nature of consumer behaviour seen as the key to economic theory. Samuelson studied such diverse fields as the dynamics and stability of economic systems, the incorporation of the theory of international trade into that of general economic equilibrium, the analysis of public goods, capital theory, welfare economics, and public expenditure. Of particular influence has been his mathematical formulation of the interaction of multiplier and accelerator effects and, in consumption analysis, his development of the theory of revealed preference.

Samuelson's lucid prose contributed to the popularity of his publications. His introductory textbook, *Economics* (1948), is considered a classic. *The Collected Scientific Papers of Paul A. Samuelson* was published in five volumes between 1966 and 1986. Samuelson was a columnist for *Newsweek* from 1966 to 1981. He was the coauthor of the textbooks *Microeconomics* and *Macroeconomics*, both first published in 1989.

Paul Samuelson. Bernard Gotfryd/Premium Archive/Getty Images

CHAPTER FORTY

HERBERT ALEXANDER SIMON

(b. June 15, 1916, Milwaukee, Wisconsin, U.S.—
d. February 9, 2001, Pittsburgh, Pennsylvania)

The American social scientist Herbert Alexander Simon was known for his contributions to a number of fields, including psychology, mathematics, statistics, and operations research, all of which he synthesized in a key theory that earned him the 1978 Nobel Prize in Economic Sciences. Simon and his longtime collaborator Allen Newell won the 1975 A.M. Turing Award, the highest honour in computer science, for their "basic contributions to artificial intelligence, the psychology of human cognition, and list processing."

Simon graduated from the University of Chicago in 1936 and earned a doctorate in political science there in 1943. After holding various posts in political science, he became a professor of administration and psychology at the Carnegie Institute of Technology (now Carnegie Mellon University) in 1949, later becoming the Richard King Mellon University Professor of Computer Science and Psychology there.

He is best known for his work on the theory of corporate decision making known as "behaviourism." In his influential book *Administrative Behavior* (1947), Simon sought to replace the highly simplified classical approach to economic modeling—based on a concept of the single decision-making, profit-maximizing entrepreneur—with an approach that recognized multiple factors that contribute to decision making. According to Simon, this theoretical framework provides a more realistic understanding of a world in which decision making can affect prices and outputs.

Crucial to this theory is the concept of "satisficing" behaviour—achieving acceptable economic objectives while minimizing complications and risks—as contrasted with the traditional emphasis on maximizing profits. Simon's theory thus offers a way to consider the psychological aspects of decision making that classical economists have tended to ignore.

Later in his career, Simon pursued means of creating artificial intelligence through computer technology. He wrote several books on computers, economics, and management, and in 1986 he won the U.S. National Medal of Science.

CHAPTER FORTY-ONE

Leonid Hurwicz

(b. August 21, 1917, Moscow, Russia—d. June 24, 2008, Minneapolis, Minnesota, U.S.)

Leonid Hurwicz was a Russian-born American economist who, with Eric Stark Maskin and Roger Bruce Myerson, received a share of the 2007 Nobel Prize for Economics for his formulation of mechanism design theory, a microeconomic model of resource allocation that attempts to produce the best outcome for market participants under nonideal conditions.

Hurwicz's parents fled their native Poland for Moscow, where Leonid was born, to escape the ravages of World War I. Fearing persecution from the newly installed Soviet government, the family returned to Poland in 1919. Hurwicz earned a law degree at the University of Warsaw in 1938. He continued his education at the London School of Economics and the Graduate Institute of International Studies in Geneva, Switzerland, but the outbreak of World War II forced him to emigrate to the United States by way of Portugal. After serving as a research assistant for Paul Samuelson at the Massachusetts Institute of Technology and for Oskar Lange at the University of Chicago, Hurwicz took a number of teaching positions before settling at the University of Minnesota in 1951. He remained there for the rest of his career, retiring from full-time teaching in

1988 but continuing as professor emeritus.

As described by Hurwicz, mechanism design theory addresses the gap in knowledge that exists between buyers and sellers. In ideal conditions, all parties have equal information about the pricing of goods within markets. In real world conditions, however, information asymmetry prevents buyers from knowing how much a seller should charge and limits the ability of sellers to determine how much a buyer will pay. The "mechanism" of mechanism design is a specialized game in which participants submit messages to a central point and a rule determines the allocation of resources based on those messages. As a result of his study of mechanism design, Hurwicz concluded that the most efficient market system for both buyers and sellers is the double auction.

Leonid Hurwicz. © AP Images

CHAPTER FORTY-TWO

JAMES TOBIN

(b. March 5, 1918, Champaign, Illinois, U.S.—d. March 11, 2002, New Haven, Connecticut)

James Tobin was an American economist whose contributions to the theoretical formulation of investment behaviour offered valuable insights into financial markets. His work earned him the Nobel Prize in Economic Sciences in 1981.

After taking degrees from Harvard University (B.A., 1939; Ph.D., 1947), Tobin spent 1941–42 as an economist with the Office of Price Administration in Washington, D.C. During World War II he served in the Naval Reserve, rising to second in command of the destroyer USS *Kearney*. In 1950 he joined the faculty of Yale University, where in 1957 he became the Sterling Professor of Economics. In addition to teaching, he served as director of the Cowles Foundation for Research in Economics from 1955 to 1961 and again from 1964 to 1965.

Tobin, regarded by many as the most distinguished American Keynesian economist, argued that monetary policy is effective in only one area—capital investment—and that interest rates are an important factor in capital investment but not the only one. He introduced "Tobin's q," the ratio of the market value of an asset to its replacement cost. If an asset's q is greater than one, then new investment in similar assets will be profitable.

Tobin served as an adviser to Democratic presidential candidate George McGovern in 1972. Like many economists across the political spectrum, he pointed out the harmful consequences of government policies, such as the effect of a high minimum wage on the job prospects of inner-city youths. Tobin once wrote: "We should be especially suspicious of interventions that seem both inefficient and inequitable, for example, rent controls in New York or Moscow or Mexico City, or price supports and irrigation subsidies benefiting affluent farmers, or low-interest loans to well-heeled students."

CHAPTER FORTY-THREE

Franco Modigliani

(b. June 18, 1918, Rome, Italy—d. September 25, 2003, Cambridge, Massachusetts, U.S.)

The Italian-born American economist and educator Franco Modigliani received the Nobel Prize in Economic Sciences in 1985 for his work on household savings and the dynamics of financial markets.

Modigliani was the son of a Jewish physician. He initially studied law, but he fled fascist Italy in 1939 for the United States and became an American citizen in 1946. He studied economics at the New School for Social Research and obtained a doctorate there in 1944. Modigliani then taught at a number of American universities, and he joined the faculty of the Massachusetts Institute of Technology in 1962, becoming professor emeritus in 1988.

Modigliani was awarded the Nobel Prize for his pioneering research in several fields of economic theory that had practical applications. One of these was his analysis of personal savings, termed the life-cycle theory. The theory posits that individuals build up a store of wealth during their younger working lives not to pass on these savings to their descendents but to consume during their own old age. The theory helped explain the varying rates of savings in societies with relatively younger or older populations and proved useful in predicting the future effects of various pension plans.

Modigliani also did important research with the American economist Merton Howard Miller on financial markets, particularly on the respective effects that a company's financial structure (e.g., the structure and size of its debt) and its future earning potential will have on the market value of its stock. They found, in the so-called Modigliani-Miller theorem, that the market value of a company depends primarily on investors' expectations of what the company will earn in the future; the company's debt-to-equity ratio is of lesser importance. This dictum gained general acceptance by the 1970s, and the technique Modigliani invented for calculating the value of a company's expected future earnings became a basic tool in corporate decision making and finance. Modigliani's autobiography, *Adventures of an Economist*, was published in 2001.

CHAPTER FORTY-FOUR

JAMES MCGILL BUCHANAN

(b. October 2, 1919, Murfreesboro, Tennessee, U.S.)

The American economist and educator James McGill Buchanan received the Nobel Prize for Economics in 1986 for his development of the "public-choice theory," a unique method of analyzing economic and political decision making.

Buchanan attended Middle Tennessee State College (B.S., 1940), the University of Tennessee (M.A., 1941), and—after five years in the navy—the University of Chicago (Ph.D., 1948). He taught at a number of universities from 1950 to 1969. From 1969 to 1983 he was Distinguished Professor of Economics at the Virginia Polytechnic Institute, and starting in 1983 he held that title at George Mason University in Fairfax, Virginia, later becoming emeritus.

Buchanan wrote a number of significant books—both with others and alone—the best known of which is *The Calculus of Consent: Logical Foundations of Constitutional Democracy* (1962), with Gordon Tullock. In this and other books, Buchanan discussed the politician's self-interest and other social (that is, noneconomic) forces that affect governmental economic policy.

CHAPTER FORTY-FIVE

JOHN CHARLES HARSANYI

(b. May 29, 1920, Budapest, Hungary—
d. August 9, 2000, Berkeley, California, U.S.)

John Charles Harsanyi was a Hungarian-American economist who shared the 1994 Nobel Prize in Economic Sciences with John Forbes Nash, Jr., and Reinhard Selten for helping to develop game theory, a branch of mathematics that attempts to analyze situations involving conflicting interests and to formulate appropriate choices and behaviours for the competitors involved.

Of Jewish descent, Harsanyi narrowly escaped deportation to a forced-labour unit during World War II. After the war he received a doctorate in philosophy from the University of Budapest (1947), where he later taught sociology. An opponent of the country's communist government, Harsanyi fled to Austria in 1950 and later that year immigrated to Australia. He attended Sydney University (M.A., 1953), studying economics, and then immigrated to the United States, where he attended Stanford University (Ph.D., 1959). From 1964 he was a professor at the Haas School of Business of the University of California, Berkeley.

Harsanyi built on the work of Nash, who had established the mathematical principles of game theory. He enhanced Nash's equilibrium model by introducing the predictability of rivals' action based on the chance that they would choose one move or countermove over another. Harsanyi was also an ethics scholar who conducted formal investigations on appropriate behaviour and correct social choices among competitors.

CHAPTER FORTY-SIX

LAWRENCE ROBERT KLEIN

(b. September 14, 1920, Omaha, Nebraska, U.S.)

The American economist Lawrence Robert Klein won the 1980 Nobel Prize in Economic Sciences for his work in developing macroeconometric models for national, regional, and world economies.

After graduating from the University of California, Berkeley, in 1942, Klein studied under the economist Paul Samuelson at the Massachusetts Institute of Technology, taking a Ph.D. in 1944. From 1944 to 1947 he was involved in econometric research at the University of Chicago, and from 1948 to 1950 he was on the staff of the National Bureau of Economic Research. Subsequently he was associated with the Survey Research Center of the University of Michigan in 1949–54, the Institute of Statistics at the University of Oxford in 1954–58, and the Wharton School of the University of Pennsylvania from 1958. From 1968 to 1991 he was Benjamin Franklin Professor of Economics and Finance (later emeritus) at the Wharton School.

Klein was one of the pioneers in building macroeconomic models. One of his earliest successes was in forecasting economic conditions at the end of World War II. Whereas many economists speculated that the war's end would bring another depression, Klein predicted that the unsatisfied demand for consumer goods throughout the war, combined with the purchasing power of returning soldiers, would likely prevent a depression; his prediction was right.

Klein's research produced a series of increasingly detailed and sophisticated models of economic activity. The Wharton Models found wide use in forecasting gross national product, exports, investment, and consumption. A more ambitious effort, the LINK project, incorporated data gathered from a large number of industrialized, centrally planned, and developing countries to forecast trade and capital movements and to test the effects of proposed changes in political and economic policies. The project is discussed in the 1995 book *Economics, Econometrics and the LINK*, edited by Manoranjan Dutta.

CHAPTER FORTY-SEVEN

DOUGLASS CECIL NORTH

(b. November 5, 1920, Cambridge, Massachusetts, U.S.)

The American economist Douglass Cecil North was a corecipient, with Robert William Fogel, of the 1993 Nobel Prize in Economic Sciences. The two were recognized for their pioneering work in cliometrics—also called "new economic history"—the application of economic theory and statistical methods to the study of history.

North studied economics at the University of California, Berkeley (B.A., 1942; Ph.D., 1952). From 1950 he taught economics at the University of Washington, leaving in 1983 to join the faculty of Washington University (St. Louis, Missouri). From 1960 to 1966 he was director of the Institute for Economic Research, and from 1967 to 1987 he was director of the National Bureau of Economic Research. He also acted as economic consultant to the governments of Russia, Argentina, Peru, and the Czech Republic. He was elected a fellow of the British Academy in 1996. From 1995 he was a visiting distinguished scholar and fellow at the Hoover Institution at Stanford University.

North's work was primarily theoretical. He argued that technical innovations alone are insufficient to propel economic development: in order for a market economy to flourish, certain legal and social institutions, such as property rights, must be in place.

CHAPTER FORTY-EIGHT

THOMAS CROMBIE SCHELLING

(b. April 14, 1921, Oakland, California, U.S.)

The American economist Thomas Crombie Schelling shared the 2005 Nobel Prize in Economic Sciences with Robert Aumann. Schelling specialized in the application of game theory to cases in which adversaries must repeatedly interact, especially in international trade, treaties, and conflicts. The cowinners were cited "for having enhanced our understanding of conflict and cooperation through game-theory analysis."

Having studied economics at the University of California, Berkeley (A.B., 1944), and Harvard University (Ph.D., 1951), Schelling began his career working for federal agencies and programs such as the U.S. Bureau of the Budget (1945–46), the Marshall Plan in Europe (1948–50), and the Executive Office of the President (1951–53). He took his first academic appointment in economics at Yale University (1953–58) before moving to Harvard University (1958–90) and subsequently to the University of Maryland (from 1990).

Schelling was also a senior staff member of the RAND Corporation (1958–59), where his analysis of the nuclear arms race between the United States and the Soviet Union led to his publication of *The Strategy of Conflict* (1960). His book promoted game theory as the principal mathematical technique for the social sciences. Among his insights were the efficacy of voluntarily limiting one's options in order to make the remaining ones more credible, that uncertain retaliation can be a greater deterrent than certain retaliation, and that the ability to retaliate is more of a deterrent than the ability to resist an attack—i.e., a country's best defense against nuclear war is the protection of its weapons rather than its people.

Schelling's idea of limited or graduated reprisals—which he later set out in *Arms and Influence* (1966)—was adopted by the United States in 1965 as Operation Rolling Thunder, which involved the bombing of selected targets in North Vietnam in the expectation that it would deter the North Vietnamese from continuing the war. When this failed to deter North Vietnam, the bombing campaign was escalated, in spite of Schelling's advice that the bombing should be abandoned if it did not succeed in the first three weeks.

While at Harvard, Schelling applied game theory to international trade negotiations, which led to two highly influential books: *Micromotives and Macrobehavior* (1978) and *Choice and Consequence* (1984).

Schelling was elected president of the American Economic Association in 1991, and, in his presidential address *Some Economics of Global Warming* (1992), he advanced an argument in favour of a carbon tax. He returned to the subject in 2002 with a controversial article in *Foreign Affairs* in which he argued that Pres. George W. Bush's rejection of the Kyoto Protocol was justified on the grounds that the link between greenhouse gases and global warming was unproven and that such a multinational accord would be unenforceable. He was one of eight experts who drafted the United Nations' Consensus of Copenhagen (2003), which suggested global priorities for the next millennium—reduction of greenhouse gases (17) falling far below treating and eradicating AIDS (1), fighting global malnutrition (2), and eliminating customs barriers (3).

Chapter Forty-Nine

Gerard Debreu

(b. July 4, 1921, Calais, France—
d. December 31, 2004, Paris)

The French-born American economist Gerard Debreu won the 1983 Nobel Prize in Economic Sciences for his fundamental contribution to the theory of general equilibrium.

In 1950 Debreu joined the Cowles Commission for Research in Economics (now the Cowles Foundation for Research in Economics) at the University of Chicago, moving with the commission to Yale University in New Haven, Connecticut, in 1955. He received a doctorate in economics from the University of Paris in 1956. He later became a professor of economics (1962) and mathematics (1975) at the University of California, Berkeley, where he taught until 1991. Debreu became a U.S. citizen in 1975.

Debreu's classic monograph, *Theory of Value: An Axiomatic Analysis of Economic Equilibrium*, was published in 1959. In it Debreu provided the mathematical underpinnings for the phenomenon of equilibrium in supply and demand that was first articulated (as the "invisible hand" that leads self-seeking individuals unwittingly to aid society) by Adam Smith in 1776. Debreu also developed methods by which to analyze the factors that influence equilibrium.

The recipient of numerous awards, Debreu was made an officer of the French Legion of Honour in 1976 and was elected a member of the National Academy of Sciences in 1977.

CHAPTER FIFTY

KENNETH JOSEPH ARROW

(b. August 23, 1921, New York, New York, U.S.)

The American economist Kenneth Joseph Arrow is known for his contributions to welfare economics and to general economic equilibrium theory. He was cowinner (with Sir John Richard Hicks) of the Nobel Prize in Economic Sciences in 1972. Perhaps his most startling thesis (built on elementary mathematics) was the "impossibility theorem" (or "Arrow's theorem"), which holds that, under certain conditions of rationality and equality, it is impossible to guarantee that a ranking of societal preferences will correspond to rankings of individual preferences when more than two individuals and alternative choices are involved.

In one of his earliest articles, published in 1951, Arrow showed that a competitive economy in equilibrium is efficient. Furthermore, he demonstrated that an efficient allocation could be reached if a government uses lump-sum taxes to transfer wealth and then lets the market work toward equilibrium. One implication of his findings is that, if a government chooses to redistribute income, it should do so directly rather than through price regulations that could hamper the free market. Arrow's early work on equilibrium still stands as one of the reasons many economists oppose price controls.

After receiving a Ph.D. from Columbia University in 1951, Arrow taught at the University of Chicago (1948–49), at Stanford University (1949–68), and at Harvard University (1968–79). In 1979 he returned to Stanford University as Joan Kenney Professor of Economics and Professor of Operations Research. Arrow became professor emeritus at Stanford in 1991.

Arrow received numerous honours and awards, including the John von Neumann Theory Prize (1986), for notable contributions to operations research and management science, and the National Medal of Science (2004), the highest scientific honour in the United States. He has also been a fellow of several academic societies, including the Econometric Society, the American Economic Association (AEA), the Institute of Mathematical Statistics, and the American Association for the Advancement of Science.

Kenneth Joseph Arrow. Bloomberg/Getty Images

CHAPTER FIFTY-ONE

MERTON HOWARD MILLER

(b. May 16, 1923, Boston, Massachusetts, U.S.—
d. June 3, 2000, Chicago, Illinois)

Merton Howard Miller was an American economist who, with Harry Markowitz and William Forsyth Sharpe, won the Nobel Prize in Economic Sciences in 1990. His contribution (and that of his colleague Franco Modigliani, who received the Nobel Prize in Economic Sciences in 1985), known as the Modigliani-Miller theorem, greatly advanced the field of finance theory.

Miller attended Harvard University (B.A., 1944), worked at the U.S. Treasury Department, and then graduated from Johns Hopkins University in Baltimore, Maryland (Ph.D., 1952). He taught at the Carnegie Institute of Technology (now Carnegie Mellon University) in Pittsburgh, Pennsylvania, until 1961, when he accepted a position as a professor of finance at the University of Chicago's Graduate School of Business Administration.

Miller built upon the work of Markowitz (whose "portfolio theory" established that wealth can best be invested in assets that vary in terms of risk and expected return) and Sharpe (who developed the "capital asset pricing model" to explain how securities prices reflect risks and potential returns). The explains the relationship between a company's capital asset structure and dividend policy and its market value and cost of capital;

the theorem demonstrates that how a manufacturing company funds its activities is less important than the profitability of those activities.

Miller was recognized as one of the most important developers of theoretical and empirical analysis in the field of corporate finance. In addition to being the business school's Robert R. McCormick Distinguished Service Professor, Miller served as a director (1990–2000) of the Chicago Mercantile Exchange.

CHAPTER FIFTY-TWO

ROBERT MERTON SOLOW

(b. August 23, 1924, Brooklyn, New York, U.S.)

The American economist Robert Merton Solow was awarded the 1987 Nobel Prize in Economic Sciences for his important contributions to theories of economic growth.

Solow received a B.A. (1947), an M.A. (1949), and a Ph.D. (1951) from Harvard University. He began teaching economics at the Massachusetts Institute of Technology (MIT) in 1949, becoming professor of economics there in 1958 and professor emeritus in 1995. He also served on the Council of Economic Advisers in 1961–62 and was a consultant to that body from 1962 to 1968.

In the 1950s Solow developed a mathematical model illustrating how various factors can contribute to sustained national economic growth. Contrary to traditional economic thinking, he showed that advances in the rate of technological progress do more to boost economic growth than do capital accumulation and labour increases.

In his 1957 article "Technical Change and the Aggregate Production Function," Solow observed that about half of economic growth cannot be accounted for by increases in capital and labour. He attributed this unaccounted-for portion—now called the "Solow residual"—to technological innovation. From the 1960s on, Solow's studies helped persuade governments to channel their funds into technological research and development to spur economic growth. A Keynesian, Solow was a witty critic of economists ranging from interventionists such as John Kenneth Galbraith to free marketers such as Milton Friedman. He was awarded the National Medal of Science in 1999.

… CHAPTER FIFTY-THREE

ROBERT WILLIAM FOGEL

(b. July 1, 1926, New York, New York, U.S.)

The American economist Robert William Fogel was awarded, with Douglass Cecil North, the Nobel Prize for Economics in 1993. The two were cited for having developed cliometrics, the application of statistical analysis to the study of economic history.

Fogel attended Cornell University (B.A., 1948), Columbia University (M.A., 1960), and Johns Hopkins University (Ph.D., 1963); he later received M.A. degrees from the University of Cambridge (1975) and Harvard University (1976). After teaching at Johns Hopkins and the University of Rochester, he joined the faculty of the University of Chicago (1964). He later accepted a position at Harvard (1975–81), after which he returned to Chicago.

Fogel first attracted attention in the early 1960s with his statistical analysis of the impact of railroads on 19th-century American economic development. Contrary to the thinking of the time, he argued that the building of railroads in the United States had contributed far less than had been believed to the overall growth of the economy. The publication in 1974 of *Time on the Cross: The Economics of American Negro Slavery*, which he wrote with Stanley L. Engerman, generated considerable controversy because it contended that slavery had been a profitable enterprise that had collapsed for political—rather than economic—reasons. The resulting furor over this theory caused Fogel to write a defense of his work, *Without Consent or Contract: The Rise and Fall of American Slavery* (1989), which included a moral condemnation of slavery and clarified his earlier research.

CHAPTER FIFTY-FOUR

VERNON SMITH

(b. January 1, 1927, Wichita, Kansas, U.S.)

The American economist Vernon Smith was a corecipient of the Nobel Prize in Economic Sciences in 2002 for his use of laboratory experiments in economic analysis, which laid the foundation for the field of experimental economics. He shared the award with Israeli-born psychologist Daniel Kahneman.

Smith studied electrical engineering at the California Institute of Technology (Caltech; B.S., 1949) then switched to economics at the University of Kansas (M.A., 1951) and Harvard (Ph.D., 1955). Smith taught and did research at Purdue University (1955–67), Brown University (1967–68), the University of Massachusetts (1968–75), Caltech (1973–75), and the University of Arizona (1975–2001), where he was Regents' Professor of Economics from 1988. In 2001 he was named professor of economics and law at George Mason University in Fairfax, Virginia. Much of Smith's commercial work was related to the deregulation of energy in the United States, Australia, and New Zealand. He served on the editorial boards of several publications and wrote extensively on subjects ranging from capital theory and finance to natural resource economics and experimental economics.

Smith's early work was inspired by the classroom experiments of his teacher at Harvard, E.H.

Chamberlain, who tested the neoclassical theory of perfect competition. Smith improved on the process of testing the fundamental economic theory that under perfect competition the market price of any product or service establishes an equilibrium between supply and demand at the level where the value assigned by a marginal buyer is equal to that of a marginal seller. The results of Smith's experiments, published in 1962, involved the random designation of the roles of buyers and sellers with different and uninformed valuations of a commodity, expressed as a lowest acceptable selling price and highest acceptable buying price. He was able to determine the theoretical equilibrium, or acceptable market price. Unexpectedly, the prices obtained in the laboratory were close to the theoretical values. Many of his experiments focused on the outcome of public auctions; he showed that the way in which the bidding was organized affected the selling price. Smith also devised "wind-tunnel tests," where trials of new alternative market designs, such as those for a deregulated industry, could be tested.

CHAPTER FIFTY-FIVE

HARRY MARKOWITZ

(b. August 24, 1927, Chicago, Illinois, U.S.)

The American finance and economics educator Harry Markowitz was a cowinner (with Merton Howard Miller and William Forsyth Sharpe) of the 1990 Nobel Prize in Economic Sciences for theories on evaluating stock-market risk and reward and on valuing corporate stocks and bonds.

Markowitz studied at the University of Chicago (Ph.B., 1947; M.A., 1950; Ph.D., 1954) and then was on the research staff of the RAND Corporation in Santa Monica, California (1952–60, 1961–63), where he met Sharpe. He then held various positions with Consolidated Analysis Centers, Inc. (1963–68), the University of California, Los Angeles (1968–69), Arbitrage Management Company, (1969–72), and IBM's T.J. Watson Research Center (1974–83) before becoming a professor of finance at Baruch College of the City University of New York. In 1994 he became a research professor of economics at the University of California, San Diego.

The research that earned Markowitz the Nobel Prize involved his "portfolio theory," which sought to prove that a diversified, or "optimal," portfolio—that is, one that mixes assets so as to maximize return and minimize risk—could be practical. His techniques for measuring the level of risk associated with various assets and his methods for mixing assets became routine investment procedures. He also developed a computer language called Simscript, used to write economic-analysis programs.

CHAPTER FIFTY-SIX

JOHN FORBES NASH, JR.

(b. June 13, 1928, Bluefield, West Virginia, U.S.)

The American mathematician John Forbes Nash, Jr., was awarded the 1994 Nobel Prize in Economic Sciences for his landmark work, first begun in the 1950s, on the mathematics of game theory. He shared the Nobel Prize with the Hungarian American economist John Charles Harsanyi and the German mathematician Reinhard Selten.

In 1948 Nash received bachelor's and master's degrees in mathematics from the Carnegie Institute of Technology (now Carnegie-Mellon University) in Pittsburgh, Pennsylvania. Two years later, at age 22, he completed his doctorate at Princeton University, publishing his influential thesis "Non-cooperative Games" in the journal *Annals of Mathematics*. He joined the faculty of the Massachusetts Institute of Technology in 1951 but resigned in the late 1950s after bouts of mental illness. He then began an informal association with Princeton.

Nash established the mathematical principles of game theory, a branch of mathematics that examines the rivalries among competitors with mixed interests. Known as the Nash solution or the Nash equilibrium, his theory attempted to explain the dynamics of threat and action among competitors. Despite its practical limitations, the Nash solution was widely applied by business strategists.

A film version of Nash's life, *A Beautiful Mind* (2001), based on Sylvia Nasar's 1998 biography of the same name, won an Academy Award for best picture. It portrays Nash's long struggle with schizophrenia.

John Forbes Nash, Jr. Getty Images

CHAPTER FIFTY-SEVEN

ROBERT AUMANN

(b. June 8, 1930, Frankfurt am Main, Germany)

The Israeli mathematician Robert Aumann shared the 2005 Nobel Prize in Economic Sciences with Thomas Crombie Schelling. Aumann's primary contribution to economics involved the analysis of repeated noncooperative encounters, a subject in the mathematical discipline of game theory. The cowinners were cited "for having enhanced our understanding of conflict and cooperation through game-theory analysis."

Aumann immigrated to the United States with his family in 1938. He was educated at the City College of New York (B.S., 1950) and the Massachusetts Institute of Technology (S.M., 1952; Ph.D., 1955), followed by postdoctoral work at Princeton University. In 1956 he moved to Israel, where he was a member of the mathematics faculty at the Hebrew University of Jerusalem until his retirement in 2000.

Aumann employed a mathematical approach to show that long-term social interaction could be analyzed using formal noncooperative game theory. Through his methodologies and analyses of so-called infinitely repeated games, he identified the outcomes that could be sustained in long-term relations and demonstrated the prerequisites for cooperation in situations where there are many participants, infrequent interaction, or the potential for a break in relations and when participants' actions lack transparency.

Aumann also extended game theory with his investigation into its cognitive foundations. He showed that peaceful cooperation is often an equilibrium solution in a repeated game even when the parties have strong short-term conflicting interests. Thus, cooperation is not necessarily dependent on goodwill or an outside arbiter. Aumann named this observation the "folk theorem."

CHAPTER FIFTY-EIGHT

REINHARD SELTEN

(b. October 5, 1930, Breslau, Germany [now Wrocław, Poland])

The German mathematician Reinhard Selten shared the 1994 Nobel Prize in Economic Sciences with John Forbes Nash, Jr., and John Charles Harsanyi for their development of game theory, a branch of mathematics that examines rivalries among competitors with mixed interests.

The son of a bookseller, Selten studied mathematics at the University of Frankfurt and graduated in 1957. He became interested in game theory in the late 1940s when he read an article about the subject in the magazine *Fortune*. Refining the research of Nash, Selten in 1965 proposed theories that distinguished between reasonable and unreasonable decisions in predicting the outcome of games. He taught at the Free University in Berlin, the University of Bielefeld, and at the University of Bonn (from 1984).

CHAPTER FIFTY-NINE

GARY STANLEY BECKER

(b. December 2, 1930, Pottsville, Pennsylvania, U.S.)

The American economist Gary Stanley Becker was awarded the Nobel Prize in Economic Sciences in 1992. He applied the methods of economics to aspects of human behaviour previously considered more or less the exclusive domain of sociology, criminology, anthropology, and demography.

Becker was educated at Princeton University and the University of Chicago, where he earned a Ph.D. in 1955. He taught economics at the University of Chicago until 1957, when he began teaching at Columbia University. In 1970 he returned to the University of Chicago as a professor of economics, and in 1983 he became a professor of sociology as well.

Becker's central premise is that rational economic choices, based on self-interest, govern most aspects of human behaviour—not just the purchasing and investment decisions traditionally thought to influence economic behaviour. In his dissertation, published in 1957 as *The Economics of Discrimination*, Becker examined racial discrimination in labour markets, concluding that discrimination has costs for both the victim and the perpetrator. In *Human Capital* (1964), he argued that an individual's investment in education and training is analogous to a company's investment in new machinery or equipment. In studies such as *A Treatise on the Family* (1981), Becker analyzed the household as a sort of factory, producing goods and services such as meals, shelter, and child care. Applying theories of production to household behaviour, he was able to make predictions about family size, divorce, and the role of women in the workplace. Subsequent work focused on such subjects as criminal behaviour and addiction. In 2000 Becker was awarded the National Medal of Science, and in 2007 he received the Presidential Medal of Freedom, the country's highest civilian award.

CHAPTER SIXTY

OLIVER EATON WILLIAMSON

(b. September 27, 1932, Superior, Wisconsin, U.S.)

The American social scientist Oliver Eaton Williamson was awarded the 2009 Nobel Prize in Economic Sciences with Elinor Ostrom "for his analysis of economic governance, especially the boundaries of the firm."

Williamson earned a bachelor's degree in management from the Massachusetts Institute of Technology Sloan School of Management (1955), a master's degree in business administration from Stanford University (1960), and a Ph.D. in economics from Carnegie Mellon University in Pittsburgh (1963). He was an assistant professor of economics at the University of California, Berkeley, until 1965, when he began teaching at the University of Pennsylvania. He was an associate professor from 1965 to 1968 and professor from 1968 to 1983. In 1983 he was named the Gordon B. Tweedy Professor of Economics of Law and Organization at Yale University, a position he held until 1988 when he returned to Berkeley. At Berkeley Williamson served as professor of the graduate school and the Edgar F. Kaiser Professor of Business, Economics, and Law (from 1998) in the Haas School of Business, becoming emeritus in 2004.

He was a consultant to various entities, including the RAND Corporation (1964–66), the U.S. Department of Justice (1967–69), the National Science Foundation (1976–77), and the Federal Trade Commission (1978–80). In 2009 Williamson and Elinor Ostrom were jointly awarded the Nobel Prize in Economic Sciences for their work in the area of economic governance, or the ways in which economic systems and hierarchical organizations operate outside the market, in terms of corporate conflict resolution. Williamson was credited with creating a new branch of economic thought—called New Institutional Economics—through his research.

Oliver Eaton Williamson. © AP Images

CHAPTER SIXTY-ONE

ROBERT ALEXANDER MUNDELL

(b. October 24, 1932, Kingston, Ontario, Canada)

The Canadian-born economist Robert Alexander Mundell received the 1999 Nobel Prize in Economic Sciences for his work on monetary dynamics and optimum currency areas.

Mundell attended the University of British Columbia (B.A., 1953), the University of Washington (M.A., 1954), the London School of Economics, and the Massachusetts Institute of Technology (Ph.D., 1956). He was a postdoctoral fellow in political economy at the University of Chicago (1956–57), where he later served as a professor of economics (1966–71) and as an editor of the *Journal of Political Economy*. In 1974 he joined the faculty of Columbia University, where he became University Professor in 2001.

In the early 1960s, while working in the research department of the International Monetary Fund, Mundell began his macroeconomic analysis of exchange rates and their effect on monetary policies. In 1961 he put forward the theory that a single currency would be viable in an economic region, or optimum currency area, in which there was free movement of labour and trade. As the first economist to study the effect of floating exchange rates (that is, allowing market forces to determine the exchange rate rather than having government try to fix its value in terms of another currency or commodity), Mundell introduced foreign trade and capital movements into earlier closed-economy models to show that it was the extent of international capital mobility that influenced stabilization policies. He concluded that a country's rate of exchange was determined in capital markets by the willingness and desire of people to possess the currency of that country. This in turn was determined by their perception of national economic prospects, inflation, and monetary policies. Mundell's groundbreaking theories played a key role in the creation of the euro, the single currency adopted by 11 of the 15 members of the European Union on January 1, 1999. Mundell's other break with tradition was his advocacy, as early as the early 1970s, of using tight money (i.e., constraints on growth of the money supply) to reduce inflation and cuts in tax rates to give incentives that would cause the real economy to grow. Mundell served as an adviser to several governments, including the United States during Ronald Reagan's presidency, and worked for such international organizations as the World Bank.

Robert Alexander Mundell. ChinaFotoPress/Getty Images

CHAPTER SIXTY-TWO

AMARTYA SEN

(b. November 3, 1933, Santiniketan, India)

The Indian economist Amartya Sen was awarded the 1998 Nobel Prize in Economic Sciences for his contributions to welfare economics and social choice theory and for his interest in the problems of society's poorest members. Sen was best known for his work on the causes of famine, which led to the development of practical solutions for preventing or limiting the effects of real or perceived shortages of food.

Sen was educated at Presidency College in Calcutta (now Kolkata). He went on to study at Trinity College, Cambridge, where he received a B.A. (1955), an M.A. (1959), and a Ph.D. (1959). He taught economics at a number of universities in India and England, including the Universities of Jadavpur (1956–58) and Delhi (1963–71), the London School of Economics, the University of London (1971–77), and the University of Oxford (1977–88), before moving to Harvard University (1988–98), where he was professor of economics and philosophy. In 1998 he was appointed master of Trinity College, Cambridge—a position he held until 2004, when he returned to Harvard as Lamont University Professor.

Welfare economics seeks to evaluate economic policies in terms of their effects on the well-being of the community. Sen, who devoted his career to such issues, was called the "conscience of his profession." His influential monograph *Collective Choice and Social Welfare* (1970)—which addressed problems such as individual rights, majority rule, and the availability of information about individual conditions—inspired researchers to turn their attention to issues of basic welfare. Sen devised methods of measuring poverty that yielded useful information for improving economic conditions for the poor. For instance, his theoretical work on inequality provided an explanation for why there are fewer women than men in some poor countries in spite of the fact that more women than men are born and infant mortality is higher among males. Sen claimed that this skewed ratio results from the better health

Amartya Sen. Prakash Singh/AFP/Getty Images

treatment and childhood opportunities afforded boys in those countries.

Sen's interest in famine stemmed from personal experience. As a nine-year-old boy, he witnessed the Bengal famine of 1943, in which three million people perished. This staggering loss of life was unnecessary, Sen later concluded. He believed that there was an adequate food supply in India at the time but that its distribution was hindered because particular groups of people—in this case rural labourers—lost their jobs and therefore their ability to purchase the food. In his book *Poverty and Famines: An Essay on Entitlement and Deprivation* (1981), Sen showed that in many cases of famine, food supplies were not significantly reduced. Instead, a number of social and economic factors—such as declining wages, unemployment, rising food prices, and poor food-distribution systems—led to starvation among certain groups in society.

Governments and international organizations handling food crises were influenced by Sen's work. His views encouraged policy makers to pay attention not only to alleviating immediate suffering but also to finding ways to replace the lost income of the poor—as, for example, through public-works projects—and to maintain stable prices for food. A vigorous defender of political freedom, Sen believed that famines do not occur in functioning democracies because their leaders must be more responsive to the demands of the citizens. In order for economic growth to be achieved, he argued, social reforms—such as improvements in education and public health—must precede economic reform.

Sen was a member of the Encyclopædia Britannica Editorial Board of Advisors from 2005 to 2007. Sen's other writings include *Rationality and Freedom* (2002), a

INFANT MORTALITY

Infant mortality is conventionally measured as the number of deaths in the first year of life per 1,000 live births during the same year. Roughly speaking, by this measure worldwide infant mortality in the early 21st century approximated 80 per 1,000; that is, about 8 percent of newborn babies died within the first year of life.

This global average disguised great differences. In certain countries of Asia and Africa, infant mortality rates exceeded 150 and sometimes approached 200 per 1,000 (that is, 15 or 20 percent of children died before reaching the age of one year). Meanwhile, in other countries, such as Japan and Sweden, the rates were well below 10 per 1,000, or 1 percent. Generally, infant mortality is somewhat higher among males than among females.

In developing countries substantial declines in infant mortality have been credited to improved sanitation and nutrition, increased access to modern health care, and improved birth spacing through the use of contraception. In industrialized countries in which infant mortality rates were already low the increased availability of advanced medical technology for newborn—in particular, prematurely born—infants provides a partial explanation.

discussion of the social choice theory, *The Argumentative Indian: Writings on Indian History, Culture, and Identity* (2005), and *AIDS Sutra: Untold Stories from India* (2008), a collection of essays on the AIDS crisis in India.

CHAPTER SIXTY-THREE

EDMUND STROTHER PHELPS

(b. July 26, 1933, Evanston, Illinois, U.S.)

The American economist Edmund Strother Phelps was awarded the 2006 Nobel Prize in Economic Sciences for his analysis of intertemporal trade-offs in policy, especially with regard to inflation, wages, and unemployment.

In 1959 Phelps earned a Ph.D. in economics from Yale University. He later taught at several schools, including Yale and the University of Pennsylvania, before joining the faculty of Columbia University in 1971.

In the late 1960s Phelps began his prizewinning work, which challenged a long-held assumption that high levels of unemployment corresponded with low levels of inflation, and vice versa. Policy makers had assumed that expansionary fiscal and monetary policies (policies

Edmund Strother Phelps. Frederic Souloy/Gamma-Rapho/Getty Images

that expanded demand) could contain unemployment levels. While this policy approach can influence short-term fluctuations in employment, it does not affect the long-term rate. Phelps observed that price- and wage-setting behaviour is based on expectations of future conditions. He demonstrated that workers will demand higher wages when costs of living (and therefore inflation) exceed their expectations. He further proved that inflation will be contained only after employment levels reach an equilibrium point. In fact, Phelps showed that unemployment is a natural part of a balanced economy: equilibrium is achieved when the economy reaches its natural rate of unemployment.

CHAPTER SIXTY-FOUR

ELINOR OSTROM

(b. August 7, 1933, Los Angeles, California, U.S.)

The American political scientist Elinor Ostrom was awarded the 2009 Nobel Prize in Economic Sciences with Oliver Eaton Williamson "for her analysis of economic governance, especially the commons" (the natural or constructed resource systems that people have in common). She was the first woman to win the economics prize.

Ostrom earned a bachelor's degree (1954), a master's degree (1962), and a Ph.D. (1965) in political science from the University of California. She began her academic career as a visiting professor of government (1965–66) at Indiana University at Bloomington, becoming an assistant professor (1966–69), associate professor of political science (1969–74), and professor (1974–91). She cofounded the university's Workshop in Political Theory and Policy Analysis in 1973 and became the first female to chair the political science department (1980–84). Ostrom later served as a professor in the School of Public and Environmental Affairs (1984–) and the Arthur F. Bentley Professor of Political Science (1991–), and from 1996 to 2006 she was codirector of the university's Center for the Study of Institutions, Population, and Environmental Change. She also was a research professor and the founding director of the Center for the Study of Institutional Diversity at Arizona State University at Tempe (2006–). Throughout her career, Ostrom was a consultant for various entities, including the State of California Local Government Reform Task Force (1973–74).

In 2009 Ostrom and Williamson were jointly awarded the Nobel Prize in Economic Sciences for their work in the area of economic governance, or the ways in which economic systems and hierarchical organizations operate outside the market. Ostrom particularly focused on the ways in which common resources such as forests, irrigation systems, and oil fields can be managed without government regulation or privatization.

Elinor Ostrom. Raveendran/AFP/Getty Images

CHAPTER SIXTY-FIVE

Daniel Kahneman

(b. March 5, 1934, Tel Aviv, Israel)

The Israeli-born psychologist Daniel Kahneman was a corecipient of the Nobel Prize in Economic Sciences in 2002 for his integration of psychological research into economic science. His pioneering work examined human judgment and decision making under uncertainty. Kahneman shared the award with American economist Vernon Smith.

Kahneman attended Hebrew University (B.A., 1954) in Jerusalem and the University of California, Berkeley (Ph.D., 1961). He was a lecturer (1961–70) and a professor (1970–78) of psychology at Hebrew University; from 2000 he held a fellowship at that university's Center for Rationality. From 1993 Kahneman was the Eugene Higgins Professor of Psychology at Princeton University and a professor of public affairs at Princeton's Woodrow Wilson School of Public and International Affairs, becoming emeritus in both professorships in 2007.

Kahneman began his prizewinning research in the late 1960s. In order to increase understanding of how people make economic decisions, he drew on cognitive psychology in relation to the mental processes used in forming judgments and making choices. Kahneman's research with Amos Tversky on decision making under uncertainty resulted in the formulation of a new branch of economics, prospect theory, which was the subject of their seminal article *Prospect Theory: An Analysis of Decisions Under Risk* (1979). Previously, economists had believed that people's decisions are determined by the expected gains from each possible future scenario multiplied by its probability of occurring, but if people make an irrational judgment by giving more weight to some scenarios than to others, their decision will be different from that predicted by traditional economic theory. Kahneman's research (based on surveys and experiments) showed that his subjects were incapable of analyzing complex decision situations when the future consequences were uncertain. Instead, they relied on heuristic shortcuts, or rules of thumb, with few people evaluating their underlying probability.

Daniel Kahneman. Sean Gallup/Getty Images

CHAPTER SIXTY-SIX

WILLIAM FORSYTH SHARPE

(b. June 16, 1934, Cambridge, Massachusetts, U.S.)

The American economist William Forsyth Sharpe shared the Nobel Prize in Economic Sciences in 1990 with Harry Markowitz and Merton Howard Miller. Their early work established financial economics as a separate field of study.

Sharpe received a Ph.D. in economics from the University of California, Los Angeles, in 1961. He was influenced by the theories of Markowitz, whom he met while working at the RAND Corporation (1957–61). Later, Sharpe taught economics at the University of Washington in Seattle (1961–68) and at Stanford University from 1970 until he retired from teaching to head his own investment consulting firm, Sharpe-Russell Research (later William F. Sharpe Associates), in the 1980s. He returned to Stanford as professor of finance in 1993, becoming emeritus in 1999. In 1996 Sharpe created the portfolio advising company Financial Engines, Inc.

Sharpe received the Nobel Prize for his "capital asset pricing model," a financial model that explains how securities prices reflect potential risks and returns. Sharpe's theory showed that the market pricing of risky assets enabled them to fit into an investor's portfolio because they could be combined with less-risky investments. His theories led to the concept of "beta," a measurement of portfolio risk. Investment analysts frequently use a beta coefficient to compare the risk of one stock against the risk of the broader stock market.

CHAPTER SIXTY-SEVEN

CLIVE GRANGER

(b. September 4, 1934, Swansea, Wales—
d. May 27, 2009, San Diego, California, U.S.)

The Welsh economist Clive Granger was a corecipient of the Nobel Prize in Economic Sciences in 2003 for his development of techniques for analyzing data with common trends. He shared the award with the American economist Robert Engle.

Granger attended the University of Nottingham (B.A., 1955; Ph.D., 1959), where he became a lecturer in statistics in the mathematics department. In 1974 he became a professor at the University of California, San Diego. He wrote numerous books, covering such subjects as time series analysis and forecasting, statistical theory, and applied statistics. He retired as professor emeritus in 2003.

In his seminal work, conducted in the 1970s and '80s, Granger developed concepts and analytic methods to establish meaningful relationships between nonstationary variables, such as exchange rates and inflation rates. His adoption of long- and short-run perspectives increased understanding of the long-term changes in macroeconomic indicators where, for example, a country's annual gross domestic product might grow long term but in the short term might suffer because of a sharp rise in commodity prices or a global economic downturn. Granger demonstrated that estimated relationships between variables that changed over time could be nonsensical and misleading because the variables were wrongly perceived as having a relationship. Even where a relationship did exist, it could be a purely temporary one. Fundamental to his methods was his discovery that a specific combination of two or more nonstationary time series could be stationary, a combination for which he invented the term cointegration. Through his cointegration analysis, Granger showed that the dynamics in exchange rates and prices, for example, are driven by a tendency to smooth out deviations from the long-run equilibrium exchange rate and short-run fluctuations around the adjustment path.

CHAPTER SIXTY-EIGHT

SIR JAMES ALEXANDER MIRRLEES

(b. July 5, 1936, Minnigaff, Scotland)

The Scottish economist Sir James Alexander Mirrlees is known for his analytic research on economic incentives in situations involving incomplete, or asymmetrical, information. He shared the 1996 Nobel Prize in Economic Sciences with William Vickrey of Columbia University.

Mirrlees studied mathematics at the University of Edinburgh (M.A., 1957) and Trinity College, Cambridge (Ph.D., 1963). In 1969 he began teaching at the University of Oxford, and he moved to the University of Cambridge in 1995. One of Mirrlees's main contributions was his pathbreaking work on optimal income taxation—a progressive tax that included incentives for earning. An adviser to the British Labour Party in the 1960s and '70s (an era of higher taxes and a more centralized control of the economy), Mirrlees started his work with the assumption that the government should take money from the rich and give it to the poor.

His conclusions were surprising. Working from this assumption and making further assumptions about people's skills and the effect that tax rates have on the incentive to earn, Mirrlees computed the top marginal tax rate for high-income earners. He found that this optimal rate was not 83 percent, the top rate in Britain at the time, but instead only 20 percent. Moreover, he concluded that the marginal tax rate should be about 20 percent for everyone, which would make the optimal structure something very close to what is now called a flat tax rate. "I must confess," wrote Mirrlees, "that I had expected the rigorous analysis of income taxation in the utilitarian manner to provide arguments for high tax rates. It has not done so." Mirrlees was knighted in 1998.

CHAPTER SIXTY-NINE

Daniel Little McFadden

(b. July 29, 1937, Raleigh, North Carolina, U.S.)

The American economist Daniel Little McFadden was a cowinner (with James Joseph Heckman) of the 2000 Nobel Prize in Economic Sciences for his development of theory and methods used in the analysis of individual or household behaviour, such as understanding how people choose where to work, where to live, or when to marry.

After studying physics (B.S., 1957) and economics (Ph.D., 1962) at the University of Minnesota, McFadden taught economics at a number of institutions, including the University of California, Berkeley (1963–79), Yale University (1977–78), and the Massachusetts Institute of Technology (1978–91). In 1990 he returned to Berkeley and was named the E. Morris Cox Professor of Economics. He also served (1991–95, and again from 1996) as the director of the university's Econometrics Laboratory. The recipient of numerous awards, McFadden was given the American Economic Association John Bates Clark Medal for his contributions to economic knowledge and thought in 1975 and was elected to the National Academy of Sciences in 1981.

McFadden's work combined economic theory, statistical methods, and empirical applications toward the resolution of social problems. In 1974 he developed conditional logit (logistic) analysis, a method for determining how individuals will choose between finite alternatives in order to maximize their utility. Through the analysis of discrete choice (i.e., the choices made between a finite set of decision alternatives), McFadden's work helped predict usage rates for public transportation systems, and his statistical methods were applied to studies of labour-force participation, health care, housing (particularly for the elderly), and the environment. In the same year, he was awarded Northwestern University's Erwin Plein Nemmers Prize in Economics, the highest monetary award for outstanding achievement in the field of economics in the United States.

Daniel Little McFadden. John G. Mabanglo/AFP/Getty Images

CHAPTER SEVENTY

ROBERT EMERSON LUCAS, JR.

(b. September 15, 1937, Yakima, Washington, U.S.)

The American economist Robert Emerson Lucas, Jr., won the 1995 Nobel Prize in Economic Sciences for developing and applying the theory of rational expectations, an econometric hypothesis. Lucas found that individuals will offset the intended results of national fiscal and monetary policy by making private economic decisions based on past experiences and anticipated results. His work, which gained prominence in the mid-1970s, questioned the conclusions of John Maynard Keynes in macroeconomics and the efficacy of government intervention in domestic affairs.

Lucas attended the University of Chicago, earning degrees in history (A.B., 1959) and economics (Ph.D., 1964). He taught at Carnegie Mellon University from 1963 to 1974 before returning to Chicago to become a professor of economics in 1975.

Lucas questioned the assumptions behind the Phillips curve, which had been thought to show that a government can lower the rate of unemployment by increasing inflation. According to the Phillips curve, higher inflation causes wages to rise more quickly, thereby fooling unemployed workers into thinking that the higher nominal wages are generous when, in fact, they are simply inflation-adjusted wages. Therefore, the unemployed take jobs more quickly, and the unemployment rate falls.

Lucas argued, however, that workers cannot be fooled again and again; higher inflation will ultimately fail to lead to lower unemployment. More generally, Lucas's work led to something called the "policy ineffectiveness proposition," the idea that if people have rational expectations, policies that try to manipulate the economy by creating false expectations may introduce more "noise" into the economy but will not improve the economy's performance. Lucas is also known for his contributions to investment theory, international finance, and economic growth theory. His *Studies in Business-Cycle Theory* (1981) collects his research from the 1970s, and *Models of Business Cycles* (1987) provides an overview of his economic theory.

Lucas edited or coedited several economics journals and served for a time as president of the American Economic Association and the Econometric Society. In 2001 Lucas published *Lectures on Economic Growth*, a collection of his writings on economic growth.

Robert Emerson Lucas, Jr. © AP Images

Dale Mortensen

(b. February 2, 1939, Enterprise, Oregon, U.S.)

The American economist Dale Mortensen was a corecipient, with Peter Arthur Diamond and Christopher Antoniou Pissarides, of the 2010 Nobel Prize in Economic Sciences "for their analysis of markets with search frictions." The theoretical framework collectively developed by the three men—which describes the search activity of the unemployed, the methods by which firms recruit and formulate wages, and the effects of economic policies and regulation—became widely used in labour market analysis.

Mortensen received a bachelor's degree in economics from Willamette University in Salem, Oregon, in 1961. He continued his education at Carnegie-Mellon University, receiving a Ph.D. in economics in 1967. Even before leaving Carnegie-Mellon, Mortensen began his long affiliation with Northwestern University, where he taught economics from 1965. In 1980 he became professor of managerial economics and decision sciences at Northwestern's Kellogg School of Management, and he also served as director of mathematical models in the university's social sciences program (1982–84, 1992–2000). Mortensen was a visiting professor at several schools, including Cornell University, New York University, and the Soviet Academy of Sciences, and he served in an editorial or advisory capacity with such organizations as the American Economic Association.

Mortensen was honoured with a Nobel Prize for the work he and Pissarides did in applying Diamond's theories on markets with search costs—i.e., those where both supply and demand can exist without aiding each other, as in the housing market—to the labour market. Among other findings, Mortensen determined that rigidities in the labour market, such as the level and length of unemployment benefits, can cause unemployment because of the length of time spent by the searcher seeking the best job with the highest pay. In his book *Wage Dispersion: Why Are Similar Workers Paid Differently* (2003), Mortensen examined the reasons for pay differentials and found that they are largely the result of job search friction and cross-firm differences in wage policy and productivity.

Dale Mortensen. Getty Images

CHAPTER SEVENTY-TWO

PETER ARTHUR DIAMOND

(b. April 29, 1940, New York, New York, U.S.)

The American economist Peter Arthur Diamond was a corecipient, with Dale Mortensen and Christopher Antoniou Pissarides, of the 2010 Nobel Prize in Economic Sciences "for their analysis of markets with search frictions." The theoretical framework collectively developed by the three men—which describes the search activity of the unemployed, the methods by which firms recruit and formulate wages, and the effects of economic policies and regulation—became widely used in labour market analysis.

Diamond received a bachelor's degree in mathematics from Yale University in 1960 and a Ph.D. in economics from the Massachusetts Institute of Technology (MIT) in 1963. He was assistant professor of economics at the University of California, Berkeley, until 1966, when he returned to MIT as an associate professor. He became a full professor in 1970 and then acceded to a series of chaired positions. Diamond also acted as research associate of the National Bureau of Economic Research from 1991 and held several other academic and editorial posts.

Diamond first gained attention in the 1960s for his work on the economic ramifications of national debt. He was honoured by the Nobel committee, however, for his later analysis of frictions in markets—that is, external factors that prevent buyers or searchers from finding a suitable match. Diamond's theories challenged the classical market view in which buyers and sellers are well informed and find each other simultaneously, without costs, ensuring that supply and demand are in balance. In a groundbreaking article in 1971, he demonstrated that when buyers sought the best possible price and sellers set their price after having taken into account the costs associated with the buyer's search, the resulting price would be the same as that set by a monopolist in a corresponding market. His finding that the only equilibrium price was the monopoly price became known as the Diamond paradox. Along with Mortensen and Pissarides, Diamond then applied these concepts to the labour market to identify and explain situations in which high unemployment rates coexist with many job vacancies. In 2010–11 he was nominated three times by U.S. Pres. Barack Obama to serve on the Federal Reserve Board; in each case, however, Senate Republicans prevented a vote on his confirmation, and he eventually withdrew his name from consideration.

Peter Arthur Diamond. © AP Images

CHAPTER SEVENTY-THREE

GEORGE AKERLOF

(b. June 17, 1940, New Haven, Connecticut, U.S.)

The American economist George Akerlof won the Nobel Prize in Economic Sciences in 2001 with Michael Spence and Joseph Stiglitz for laying the foundation for the theory of markets with asymmetric information.

Akerlof studied at Yale University (B.A., 1962) and the Massachusetts Institute of Technology (Ph.D., 1966). In 1966 he began teaching at the University of California, Berkeley, becoming Goldman Professor of Economics in 1980. His research often drew from other disciplines, including psychology, anthropology, and sociology, and he played an important role in the development of behavioral economics.

Akerlof's study of markets with asymmetric information concentrated on those in which sellers of a product have more information than buyers about the product's quality. Using the example of a secondhand-car market, he demonstrated that this could lead to "adverse selection" of poor-quality products, such as a defective car known as a "lemon." In his 1970 seminal work "The Market for Lemons: Quality Uncertainty and the Market Mechanism," Akerlof explained how private or asymmetric information prevents markets from functioning efficiently and examined the consequences. He suggested that many economic institutions had emerged in the market in order to protect themselves from the consequences of adverse selection, including second-hand-car dealers who offered guarantees to increase consumer confidence. In the context of less-developed countries, Akerlof's analysis explained that interest rates were often excessive because moneylenders lacked adequate information on the borrower's creditworthiness.

CHAPTER SEVENTY-FOUR

EDWARD PRESCOTT

(b. December 26, 1940, Glens Falls, New York, U.S.)

The American economist Edward Prescott won the Nobel Prize in Economic Sciences in 2004 with Finn Erling Kydland for contributions to two areas of dynamic macroeconomics: the time consistency of economic policy and the driving forces behind business cycle fluctuations.

Prescott studied mathematics at Swarthmore College (B.A., 1962), operations research at Case Western Reserve University (M.S., 1963), and economics at Carnegie Mellon University (Ph.D., 1967). From 1966 to 1971 he taught economics at the University of Pennsylvania, and he then joined the faculty at Carnegie Mellon (1971), where he advised Kydland on his doctorate. Prescott, who also taught at the University of Minnesota and Arizona State University, was named an adviser to the Federal Reserve Bank of Minneapolis in 1980.

Prescott and Kydland, working separately and together, influenced the monetary and fiscal policies of governments and laid the basis for the increased independence of many central banks, notably those in Sweden, New Zealand, and the United Kingdom. In their seminal article *Rules Rather than Discretion: The*

Inconsistency of Optimal Plans (1977), they demonstrated how a declared commitment to a low inflation rate by policy makers might create expectations of low inflation and unemployment rates. If this monetary policy is then changed and interest rates are reduced—for example, to give a short-term boost to employment—the policy makers' (and thus the government's) credibility will be lost and conditions worsened by the "discretionary" policy. In *Time to Build and Aggregate Fluctuations* (1982), the two economists established the microeconomic foundation for business cycle analyses, demonstrating that technology changes or supply shocks, such as oil price hikes, could be reflected in investment and relative price movements and thereby create short-term fluctuations around the long-term economic growth path.

In addition to winning the Nobel Prize, Prescott was a fellow of the Brookings Institution, the Guggenheim Foundation, the Econometric Society, and the American Academy of Arts and Sciences; he was elected a member of the National Academy of Sciences in 2008.

CHAPTER SEVENTY-FIVE

MYRON SAMUEL SCHOLES

(b. January 7, 1941, Timmins, Ontario, Canada)

The Canadian-born American economist Myron Samuel Scholes is best known for work with his colleague Fischer Black on the Black-Scholes option valuation formula, which made trading more accessible by giving investors a benchmark for valuing. Scholes shared the 1997 Nobel Prize in Economic Sciences with Robert Merton, who generalized the Black-Scholes formula to make it apply to other areas of finance. (Fischer Black, who died in 1995, was ineligible for the Nobel Prize, which is not awarded posthumously.)

After attending McMaster University in Hamilton, Ontario (B.A., 1961), Scholes studied under Nobel laureate Merton Howard Miller at the University of Chicago (M.B.A., 1964; Ph.D., 1970). Scholes taught at the Massachusetts Institute of Technology (1968–73) and the University of Chicago (1973–83) before joining Stanford University in 1983 as a professor of both law and finance, becoming emeritus in 1996. He also worked with many economic and financial institutions, including the National Bureau of Economic Research; Salomon Brothers; (LTCM), which Merton cofounded in 1994; Platinum Grove Asset Management, L.P., which he cofounded in 1999; the Chicago Mercantile Exchange; and Dimensional Fund Advisors. Because of its highly leveraged positions, LTCM lost more than $4 billion in

1998. (After an Internal Revenue Service [IRS] audit found that LTCM had taken $106 million in improper deductions, the firm was liquidated in 2000.)

Before the Black-Scholes formula appeared in 1973, investors had lacked realistic means for determining the future value of an option. Though it was complex and involved many assumptions and restrictions, the formula showed that shares and call options could be combined to form a riskless portfolio. This approach was adopted by traders worldwide as the main method for valuing stock options. Merton expanded the formula to other areas of finance, such as home mortgages, and to risk management in general.

CHAPTER SEVENTY-SIX

CHRISTOPHER ALBERT SIMS

(b. October 21, 1942, Washington, D.C., U.S.)

The American economist Christopher Albert Sims was awarded the 2011 Nobel Prize in Economic Sciences with Thomas John Sargent. He and Sargent were honoured for their independent but complementary research on how changes in macroeconomic indicators such as gross domestic product (GDP), inflation, investment, and unemployment causally interact with economic "shocks," or unexpected events having at least short-term economic consequences (Sims), and with long-term government economic policy (Sargent).

Sims attended Harvard University, receiving a B.A. in mathematics in 1963 and a Ph.D. in economics in 1968. After teaching for three years at Harvard, he joined the economics faculty of the University of Minnesota, where he remained until his appointment in 1990 as Henry Ford II Professor of Economics at Yale University. In 1999 he left Yale for Princeton University, where he was a professor of economics and later Harold H. Helm '20 Professor of Economics and Banking.

Sims's Nobel Prize–winning work focused on tracing the effects on the broader economy of economic shocks such as a shift in government economic policy (e.g., a change in the prime interest rate), an increase in the price of oil, or a decline in aggregate consumption.

Sims developed a method based on a statistical tool called vector autoregression to distinguish shocks that come about as a result of other shocks (e.g., a change in the prime rate resulting from a rise in inflation) and those that occur independently. Independent shocks, called fundamental shocks, can then be interpreted using a technique called impulse-response analysis to identify their effects over time on various macroeconomic indicators. Part of the significance of Sims's approach was that it provided a means of identifying rationally expected and rationally unexpected changes in economic policy. The two kinds of changes had previously been difficult to distinguish on the basis of variations in macroeconomic indicators, which could in principle be attributed either to an unexpected policy change or to changes in private-sector behaviour undertaken in expectation of a policy change.

Christopher Albert Sims. © AP Images

CHAPTER SEVENTY-SEVEN

ROBERT ENGLE

(b. November 1942, Syracuse, New York, U.S.)

The American economist Robert Engle was a corecipient of the Nobel Prize in Economic Sciences in 2003 for his development of methods for analyzing time series data with time-varying volatility. He shared the award with Clive Granger.

Engle received an M.S. (1966) and a Ph.D. (1969) from Cornell University. He taught at the Massachusetts Institute of Technology (1969–75) before joining the University of California, San Diego (UCSD), where he became a professor of economics in 1977 and chair of the department of economics from 1990 to 1994. In 1999 he began teaching at the Stern School of Business at New York University, where he was Michael Armellino Professor of Finance. He retired from UCSD as professor emeritus and research professor in 2003. Engle also held associate editorships on several academic journals, notably the *Journal of Applied Econometrics*, of which he was coeditor from 1985 to 1989.

Engle conducted much of his prizewinning work in the 1970s and '80s, when he developed improved mathematical techniques for the evaluation and accurate forecasting of risk, which enabled researchers to test if and how volatility in one period was related to volatility in another period. This work had particular relevance in financial market analysis, in which the investment returns of an asset were assessed against its risks and in which stock prices and returns could exhibit extreme volatility. While periods of strong turbulence caused large fluctuations in prices in stock markets, these were often followed by relative calm and slight fluctuations. Inherent in Engle's autoregressive conditional heteroskedasticity (known as ARCH) model was the concept that, while most volatility is embedded in random error, its variance depends on previously realized random errors, with large errors being followed by large errors and small by small. This contrasted with earlier models wherein the random error was assumed to be constant over time. Engle's methods and the ARCH model led to a proliferation of tools for analyzing stocks and enabled economists to make more accurate forecasts.

Chapter Seventy-Eight

Michael Spence

(b. 1943, Montclair, New Jersey, U.S.)

The American economist Michael Spence won the 2001 Nobel Prize in Economic Sciences with George Akerlof and Joseph Stiglitz, for laying the foundations of the theory of markets with asymmetric information.

Spence studied at Yale University (B.A., 1966), the University of Oxford (B.A., M.A., 1968), and Harvard University (Ph.D., 1972). He taught at Harvard and at Stanford University, serving as dean of the latter's business school from 1990 to 1999.

Through his research on markets with asymmetric information, Spence developed the theory of "signaling" to show how better-informed individuals in the market communicate their information to the less-well-informed to avoid the problems associated with adverse selection. In his 1973 seminal paper "Job Market Signaling," Spence demonstrated how a college degree signals a job seeker's intelligence and ability to a prospective employer. Other examples of signaling included corporations giving large dividends to demonstrate profitability and manufacturers issuing guarantees to convey the high quality of a product.

CHAPTER SEVENTY-NINE

JOSEPH STIGLITZ

(b. February 9, 1943, Gary, Indiana, U.S.)

The American economist Joseph Stiglitz won the 2001 Nobel Prize in Economic Sciences with Michael Spence and George Akerlof, for laying the foundations of the theory of markets with asymmetric information.

After studying at Amherst College (B.A., 1964) in Massachusetts and the Massachusetts Institute of Technology (Ph.D., 1967), Stiglitz taught at several universities, including Yale, Harvard, and Stanford. He was an active member of Pres. Bill Clinton's economic policy team; a member of the U.S. Council of Economic Advisers (1993–97), of which he became chairman in June 1995; and senior vice president and chief economist of the World Bank (1997–2000). In 2001 he became professor of economics, business, and international affairs at Columbia University.

Stiglitz's research concentrated on what could be done by ill-informed individuals and operators to improve their position in a market with asymmetric information. He found that they could extract information indirectly through screening and self-selection. This point was illustrated through his study of the insurance market, in which the (uninformed) companies lacked information on the individual risk situation of their (informed) customers. The analysis showed that by offering incentives to policyholders to disclose information, insurance companies were able to divide them into different risk classes. The use of a screening process enabled companies to issue a choice of policy contracts in which lower premiums could be exchanged for higher deductibles.

Joseph Stiglitz. Bloomberg/Getty Images

CHAPTER EIGHTY

Thomas John Sargent

(b. July 19, 1943, Pasadena, California, U.S.)

The American economist Thomas John Sargent was awarded the 2011 Nobel Prize in Economic Sciences with Christopher Albert Sims. He and Sims were honoured for their independent but complementary research on how changes in macroeconomic indicators such as gross domestic product (GDP), inflation, investment, and unemployment causally interact with government economic policies (Sargent) and with economic "shocks," or unexpected events (such as a sudden rise in the price of oil) with at least short-term economic consequences (Sims).

Sargent received a B.A. degree from the University of California, Berkeley, in 1964 and a Ph.D. in economics from Harvard University in 1968. After serving in the U.S. Army as a systems analyst in the office of the assistant secretary of defense (1968–69), he taught at various universities in the United States until the early 1980s. He was a visiting scholar and later a senior fellow at the Hoover Institution at Stanford University from 1985. In the 1990s he held endowed chairs in economics at the University of Chicago and Stanford, and in 2002 he was appointed William R. Berkley Professor of Economics and Business at New York University.

In the 1970s Sargent helped to develop rational expectations theory, which holds that certain economic outcomes (e.g., commodity prices) are partly determined by what people rationally expect those outcomes to be. Sargent's Nobel Prize–winning work focused on isolating the causes and effects of changes in long-term economic policies, such as the adoption of new inflation targets or the imposition of permanent constraints on government budgets. The main challenge faced by analysts of such changes was that economic policy is influenced by the rational expectations of policy makers about future economic performance, while economic performance is influenced by the rational expectations of business leaders and investors about future economic policy. This interplay makes it difficult to determine whether (or to what extent) a given change in performance was caused by a change in policy or by a change in private-sector behaviour undertaken in expectation of a change in policy. Sargent developed a method, based on the analysis of historical data, for describing basic relations between macroeconomic indicators and expectations of economic policy that are not affected when economic policy shifts. These relations can be incorporated into mathematical models that account for historical data and reliably predict the effects of different policies in hypothetical circumstances. Sargent also applied his method in studies of historical episodes of hyperinflation and of the stagflation that characterized the U.S. and other economies in the 1970s.

Thomas John Sargent. © AP Images

CHAPTER EIGHTY-ONE

FINN ERLING KYDLAND

(b. December 1943, Ålgård, near Stavanger, Norway)

The Norwegian economist Finn Erling Kydland won the 2004 Nobel Prize in Economic Sciences with Edward Prescott, for contributions to dynamic macroeconomics, notably the time consistency of economic policy and the driving forces behind business cycles.

Kydland was educated at the Norwegian School of Economics and Business Administration (NHH; B.S., 1968) and Carnegie Mellon University in Pittsburgh (Ph.D., 1973), where Prescott advised him on his doctorate. Kydland was an assistant professor of economics at NHH (1973–78) and taught at Carnegie Mellon (1978–2004) before joining the faculty at the University of California, Santa Barbara, in 2004. He also served as a consultant research associate to the Federal Reserve banks of Dallas and Cleveland.

Kydland and Prescott, working separately and together, influenced the monetary and fiscal policies of governments and laid the basis for the increased independence of many central banks, notably those in the United Kingdom, Sweden, and New Zealand. In their seminal article "Rules Rather than Discretion: The Inconsistency of Optimal Plans" (1977), the two economists demonstrated how a declared commitment to a low inflation rate by policy makers might create expectations of low inflation and unemployment rates. If this monetary policy is then changed and interest rates are reduced—for example, to take political advantage of the prosperity generated by increased inflation or to give a short-term boost to employment—the policy makers' (and thus the government's) credibility will be lost and conditions worsened by the "discretionary" policy. In "Time to Build and Aggregate Fluctuations" (1982), the pair demonstrated that technology changes or supply shocks, such as oil price hikes, could be reflected in investment and relative price movements and thereby create short-term fluctuations around the long-term economic growth path.

CHAPTER EIGHTY-TWO

JAMES JOSEPH HECKMAN

(b. April 19, 1944, Chicago, Illinois, U.S.)

The American economist and educator James Joseph Heckman was a cowinner (with Daniel Little McFadden) of the 2000 Nobel Prize in Economic Sciences for his development of theory and methods used in the analysis of individual or household behaviour, such as understanding how people choose where to work, where to live, or when to get married. He was recognized as a leading researcher of the microevaluation of labour-market programs.

Heckman studied mathematics at Colorado College (B.A., 1965) and economics at Princeton University (M.A., 1968; Ph.D., 1971). He taught at New York University (1972) and Columbia University (1970–74) before joining (1973) the economics faculty at the University of Chicago, where he was named the Henry Schultz Distinguished Service Professor of Economics in 1995. From 1988 to 1990 he also taught at Yale University. Heckman served as a research professor for the American Bar Foundation (ABF) from 1991. From 2004 to 2008 he held the Distinguished Chair of Microeconometrics at University College London. Heckman became Professor of Science and Society at University College Dublin in 2006.

Heckman's work in selective samples led him to develop methods (such as the Heckman correction) for overcoming statistical sample-selection problems. When a sample fails to represent reality, the statistical analyses based on those samples can lead to erroneous policy decisions. The Heckman correction, a two-step statistical approach, offers a means of correcting for sampling errors.

Heckman is the author of more than 200 papers and has contributed to and edited several books, including (with Alan B. Krueger and Benjamin M. Friedman) *Inequality in America: What Role for Human Capital Policies* (2002). In 1983 he was awarded the John Bates Clark Medal by the American Economics Association, and in 1992 he was elected to the National Academy of Sciences. In 2008 he served as a policy analyst in the presidential campaign of Barack Obama.

James Joseph Heckman. Globo/Getty Images

CHAPTER EIGHTY-THREE

Robert Merton

(b. July 31, 1944, New York, New York, U.S.)

The American economist Robert Merton is known for his work on finance theory and risk management and especially for his contribution to assessing the value of stock options and other derivatives. In 1997 he shared the Nobel Prize in Economic Sciences with Myron Samuel Scholes, whose option valuation model, the Black-Scholes formula (developed with economist Fischer Black), provided the foundation for much of Merton's work. (Upon his death in 1995, Black became ineligible for the Nobel Prize, which is not awarded posthumously.)

After studying engineering mathematics at Columbia University (B.S., 1966) and applied mathematics at the California Institute of Technology (M.S., 1967), Merton turned to the study of economics at the Massachusetts Institute of Technology (Ph.D., 1970). He taught at MIT's Sloan School of Management from 1970 until 1988, when he joined the faculty of the Harvard Business School. In addition to his academic duties, he served on the editorial boards of numerous economic journals and as a principal member of Long-Term Capital Management—an investment firm he cofounded and in which Scholes was also a partner—which failed in 1998. Merton wrote many economic treatises, as well as the book *Continuous-Time Finance* (1990).

Though his research covers many areas of finance theory and economics, Merton's work on option valuation is perhaps his most influential. Prior to 1973, when Black and Scholes published their landmark formula, determining the value of stock options was extremely risky and difficult because of the nature of options, which are essentially agreements that give investors the right to either buy or sell an asset at some fixed time in the future. The challenge of an option is to predict its value at that distant time; before the Black-Scholes formula was introduced, those investing in options determined a risk premium to hedge against major financial losses. The Black-Scholes formula showed that risk premiums are not necessary for investment in stock options because such premiums are already factored into the prices of stocks. Merton used his background in mathematics to generalize the formula by relaxing certain restrictions and assumptions set by Black and Scholes, such as the rather unlikely assumption that the stock will pay no dividends. By altering the formula, Merton allowed it to apply to other financial matters, such as mortgages and student loans.

CHAPTER EIGHTY-FOUR

CHRISTOPHER ANTONIOU PISSARIDES

(b. February 20, 1948, Nicosia, Cyprus)

The British-Cypriot economist Christopher Antoniou Pissarides was a corecipient, with Peter Arthur Diamond and Dale Mortensen, of the 2010 Nobel Prize in Economic Sciences "for their analysis of markets with search frictions." The theoretical framework collectively developed by the three men—which describes the search activity of the unemployed, the methods by which firms recruit and formulate wages, and the effects of economic policies and regulation—became widely used in labour market analysis.

Pissarides grew up in Cyprus and moved to England to study at the University of Essex, where he received a B.A. (1970) and an M.A. (1971) in economics. He later earned a Ph.D. (1973) at the London School of Economics (LSE). After working briefly at the Central Bank of Cyprus, Pissarides returned to academia as a lecturer in economics at the University of Southampton. In 1976 he took a similar position at the LSE and became a full professor 10 years later. Pissarides wrote and lectured widely on labour market theory and policy, and his book *Equilibrium Unemployment Theory* (1990) became a standard text in the field. In 2002 he earned election to the British Academy, and from 2009 he also served on the executive committee of the European Economic Association.

Pissarides was honoured by the Nobel committee for his work, frequently conducted with Mortensen, that developed Diamond's theories involving frictions within search markets—cases in which buyers and sellers do not easily converge—and applied them to the job market. In the course of his research, Pissarides pioneered a coherent theoretical analysis of the dynamics of unemployment, job vacancies, and real wages, and he helped to develop the concept of matching functions. Notably, he found that the more intensely job seekers looked for employment, the more jobs companies would offer because of the ease with which they could fill those positions.

Christopher Antoniou Pissarides. Giorgio Cosulich/Getty Images

CHAPTER EIGHTY-FIVE

ERIC STARK MASKIN

(b. December 12, 1950, New York City, New York, U.S.)

The American economist Eric Stark Maskin received a share of the 2007 Nobel Prize in Economic Sciences, with Leonid Hurwicz and Roger Bruce Myerson, for his work on mechanism design theory, a specialized form of game theory that attempts to maximize gains for all parties within markets.

Maskin studied at Harvard University, earning a bachelor's degree in mathematics (1972) and a master's degree (1974) and doctorate (1976) in applied mathematics. He taught economics at the Massachusetts Institute of Technology (1977–84) before becoming a professor at Harvard University (1985–2000). In 2000

Eric Stark Maskin. Bloomberg/Getty Images

he was named a visiting lecturer at Princeton University and the Albert O. Hirschman Professor of Social Science at Princeton's Institute for Advanced Study.

With the concept of implementation theory, Maskin built on the mechanism design work of Leonid Hurwicz. Implementation theory introduced mechanisms to the market that would lead to optimal outcomes for all participants. This work had applications in the financial sector, in studies of voter behaviour, and in business management.

CHAPTER EIGHTY-SIX

ROGER BRUCE MYERSON

(b. March 29, 1951, Boston, Massachusetts, U.S.)

The American economist Roger Bruce Myerson shared, with Leonid Hurwicz and Eric Stark Maskin, the 2007 Nobel Prize in Economic Sciences for his work on mechanism design theory.

Roger Bruce Myerson. Nicholas Kamm/AFP/Getty Images

Myerson earned both bachelor's and master's degrees in applied mathematics from Harvard University in 1973. In 1976 he was awarded a doctorate from Harvard; in his thesis he examined cooperative games, a subject he explored further in his landmark 1981 paper on optimal auction design. In 1976 he took a post in the economics department at Northwestern University in Evanston, Illinois. He remained there until 2001, when he accepted a position at the University of Chicago.

At its most basic, mechanism design theory tries to simulate market conditions in such a way as to maximize gains for all parties. As buyers and sellers within a market rarely know one another's motives or ambitions, resources may be lost or misallocated because of information asymmetry. Myerson addressed this problem by proposing the revelation principle, wherein buyers are offered an incentive for truthfully reporting what they would pay for goods or services.

CHAPTER EIGHTY-SEVEN

PAUL ROBIN KRUGMAN

(b. February 28, 1953, Albany, New York, U.S.)

The American economist and journalist Paul Robin Krugman received the 2008 Nobel Prize in Economic Sciences for his work in economic geography and in identifying international trade patterns.

Krugman was awarded a B.A. from Yale University in 1974 and a Ph.D. from the Massachusetts Institute of Technology (MIT) in 1977. He served as a member of MIT's economics faculty from 1979 to 2000, leaving for a year (1982–83) to work as the chief staffer for international economics on Pres. Ronald Reagan's Council of Economic Advisers and again for a hiatus (1994–96) to teach at Stanford University. From 1979 he also worked as a research associate at the National Bureau of Economic Research. In 2000 he became a professor of economics and international affairs at the Woodrow Wilson School of Public and International Affairs at Princeton University.

Through the integration of economies of scale into general equilibrium models, Krugman furthered understanding of both the determinants of trade and the location of production in an increasingly globalized post-World War II economy. His research findings explained how the consumer's desire for variety and choice enabled countries to achieve the economies of scale required for profitable trade in similar products. This led to later research on the "new economic geography," which explained the location of jobs and businesses and the reason there was acceleration in the pace of urbanization and a population decline in rural areas.

A prolific writer, Krugman published more than 20 books and 200 papers in professional journals. Among his writings were regular magazine columns in *Slate* (1996–99) and *Fortune* (1997–99), and from 1999 he was an op-ed columnist for the *New York Times*. His books include the essay collection *The Great Unraveling: Losing Our Way in the New Century* (2003), which criticized the administration of Pres. George W. Bush; economics textbooks such as *Microeconomics* (2004) and *Macroeconomics* (2005); and nonacademic best sellers such as *The Return of Depression Economics* (1999), *The Conscience of a Liberal* (2007), and *The Return of Depression Economics and the Crisis of 2008* (2009). In addition to the Nobel Prize, Krugman received many honours, including the 1991 John Bates Clark medal, awarded to economists under age 40.

Paul Robin Krugman. Mike Clarke/AFP/Getty Images

GLOSSARY

capitalism An economic system characterized by private or corporate ownership of capital goods, by investments that are determined by private decision, and by prices, production, and the distribution of goods that are determined mainly by competition in a free market.

commodities An economic good such as a product of agriculture or mining.

communism A system in which goods are owned in common and are available to all as needed.

depression A period of low general economic activity marked especially by rising levels of unemployment.

feudalism The system of political organization prevailing in Europe from the 9th to about the 15th centuries having as its basis the relation of lord to vassal with all land held in fee and as chief characteristics homage, the service of tenants under arms and in court, wardship, and forfeiture.

flat tax A tax in which the tax rate remains constant regardless of the amount of the tax base.

free market An economic market operating by free competition.

gross domestic product The total value of the goods and services produced by the people of a nation during a year not including the value of income earned in foreign countries.

gross national product The total value of the goods and services produced by the people of a nation during a year.

inflation A continuing rise in the general price level.

laissez-faire A doctrine opposing governmental interference in economic affairs beyond the minimum necessary for the maintenance of peace and property rights.

macroeconomics A study of economics in terms of whole systems especially with reference to general levels of output and income and to the interrelations among sectors of the economy.

market The area of economic activity in which buyers and sellers come together and the forces of supply and demand affect prices.

marxism The political, economic, and social theories of Karl Marx including the belief that the struggle between social classes is a major force in history and that there should eventually be a society in which there are no classes.

materialism The theory that physical matter is the only or fundamental reality and that all being and processes and phenomena can be explained as manifestations or results of matter.

microeconomics A study of economics in terms of individual areas of activity.

monetarism The theory that physical matter is the only or fundamental reality and that all being and processes and phenomena can be explained as manifestations or results of matter.

monopoly Complete control of the entire supply of goods or of a service in a certain area or market.

socialism A way of organizing a society in which major industries are publicly owned and controlled rather than owned by individual people and companies.

totalitarianism A form of government that theoretically permits no individual freedom and that seeks to subordinate all aspects of the individual's life to the authority of the government

FOR FURTHER READING

Ferguson, Niall. *The Ascent of Money: A Financial History of the World*. New York: Penguin, 2009.

Ferguson, Niall. *The Cash Nexus: Economics and Politics from the Age of Warfare through the Age of Welfare, 1700-2000*. New York: Basic, 2002.

Friedman, Milton, and Rose D. Friedman. *Capitalism and Freedom*. Chicago: University of Chicago, 2002.

Friedman, Milton, Leonard J. Savage, and Gary S. Becker. *Milton Friedman on Economics: Selected Papers*. Chicago: University of Chicago, 2007.

Friedman, Milton. *Why Government Is the Problem: /Milton Friedman*. Stanford, Calif.: Hoover Institution on War, Revolution, and Peace, Stanford University, 1993.

Friedman, Thomas L. *The World Is Flat: A Brief History of the Twenty-first Century*. New York: Picador/Farrar, Straus and Giroux, 2007.

Galbraith, John Kenneth, and Andrea D. Williams. *The Essential Galbraith*. Boston: Houghton Mifflin, 2001.

Galbraith, John Kenneth, and James K. Galbraith. *John Kenneth Galbraith: The Affluent Society and Other Writings, 1952-1967: American Capitalism, The Great Crash, 1929, The Affluent Society, The New Industrial State*. New York, NY: Library of America, 2010.

Hayek, Friedrich A. Von, and Bruce Caldwell. *The Road to Serfdom: Text and Documents*. Chicago: University of Chicago, 2007.

Keynes, John Maynard. *The General Theory of Employment, Interest, and Money.* New York: Harcourt, Brace & World, 1964.

Krugman, Paul R. *End This Depression Now!* New York, NY: W. W. Norton, 2012.

Marx, Karl, and Eugene Kamenka. *The Portable Karl Marx.* Harmondsworth, Middlesex, England: Penguin, 1983.

Smith, Adam, and Edwin Cannan. *The Wealth of Nations.* New York, NY: Bantam Classic, 2003.

Stigler, George J. *Memoirs of an Unregulated Economist.* Chicago: University of Chicago, 2003.

Stiglitz, Joseph E. *Globalization and Its Discontents.* New York: W.W. Norton, 2003.

INDEX

A

Akerlof, George, 164–165, 174, 175
Allais, Maurice, 85–86
Arrow, Kenneth Joseph, 73, 117–118
asymmetric information, 164, 174, 175
Aumann, Robert, 114, 131–132
Austrian school of economics, 28, 32–33, 34

B

Bakunin, Mikhail Alexandrovich, 22–23
Becker, Gary Stanley, 134–135
behaviourism, 100–101
Black, Fischer, 168, 184, 185
Black-Scholes formula, 168, 184, 185
Böhm-Bawerk, Eugen von, 32–33, 34
Buchanan, James McGill, 108

C

Chamberlin, Edward Hastings, 64–65, 125–126
cliometrics, 113, 123
Coase, Ronald, 45, 82–83
Cochrane, Andrew, 3
Commons, John Rogers, 41–42
communism, 17, 18–19, 20
Communist Manifesto, The, 14, 18

D

Das Kapital, 14, 21
Debreu, Gerard, 116
deficit financing, 51
Diamond, Peter Arthur, 160, 161, 162–163, 186, 187

E

econometrics, 53, 54, 71, 74, 87, 111, 158
Economic Consequences of the Peace, The, 50
Engels, Friedrich, 14, 17, 18–19, 20, 21, 22, 23
Engle, Robert, 152, 172–173
equilibrium, theory of, 116, 117, 126, 145

F

Feuerbach, Ludwig, 16
Fogel, Robert William, 113, 123–124
Friedman, Milton, 90–93, 122
Frisch, Ragnar, 53–54, 71

G

Galbraith, John Kenneth, 78–79, 122
game theory, 109, 114, 129, 131–132, 133, 188

General Theory of Employment, Interest and Money, The, 47, 50–51, 60
Granger, Clive, 152–153, 172

H

Haavelmo, Trygve, 87
Harrod, Sir Roy, 66
Harsanyi, John Charles, 109–110, 129, 133
Hayek, Friedrich August von, 55, 59–63, 91
Heckman, James Joseph, 156, 182–183
Heckscher, Eli, 57, 58
Hegel, George Wilhelm Friedrich, 16
Hicks, Sir John Richard, 73, 85, 89, 117
human capital, 69, 70
Hume, David, 2, 3, 4–5
Hurwicz, Leonid, 102–103, 189

I

implementation theory, 189
Industrial Revolution, 18
infant mortality, rates of, 143
Inquiry into the Nature and Causes of the Wealth of Nations, An, 1, 3, 4, 5–8, 11
International Working Men's Association, 21, 22, 23

J

Jevons, William Stanley, 26–27, 28, 31

K

Kahneman, Daniel, 125, 148–149
Kantorovich, Leonid Vitalyevich, 80, 88–89
Keynes, John Maynard, 35, 47–52, 57, 58, 59, 60, 66, 73, 76, 93, 94, 104, 122, 158
Klein, Lawrence Robert, 111–112
Knight, Frank H., 55, 64
Koopmans, Tjalling Charles, 80–81, 88
Krugman, Paul Robin, 192–193
Kuznets, Simon, 67–68
Kydland, Finn Erling, 166–167, 180–181

L

laissez-faire, 7, 9, 10–11, 13, 50
Leontief, Wassily, 74–75
Leontief Paradox, 75
Lewis, Sir Arthur, 69, 97
life-cycle theory, 106
linear programming, 88
Lucas, Robert Emerson, Jr., 158–159

M

macroeconomics, 53, 54, 58, 66, 93, 111, 158, 166, 177, 180
marginal productivity theory, 35
marginal utility theory, 26, 28, 31
Markowitz, Harry, 119, 127–128, 150
Marshall, Alfred, 30–31, 45, 48, 50

INDEX

Marx, Karl, 13, 14–23, 24, 28, 33, 73
Marxism, 14, 89
Maskin, Eric Stark, 102, 188–189, 190
McFadden, Daniel Little, 156–157, 182
Meade, James Edward, 57, 76–77
mechanism design theory, 103, 191
Menger, Carl, 26, 28–29, 32, 34
Merton, Robert, 168, 184–185
Mill, John Stuart, 10–11, 31
Miller, Merton Howard, 107, 119–120, 127, 150, 168
Mirrlees, Sir James Alexander, 95, 154–155
Mises, Ludwig von, 59–60
Mitchell, Wesley Clair, 43–44
Modigliani, Franco, 106–107, 119
Modigliani-Miller theorem, 107, 119
monetarism, 93
monetary theory, 35
money supply, 91
Mortensen, Dale, 160–161, 162, 163, 186, 187
Mundell, Robert Alexander, 138–139
Myerson, Roger Bruce, 102, 188, 190–191
Myrdal, Gunnar, 55–56, 59, 62

N

Nash, John Forbes, Jr., 109, 129–130, 133
new institutional economics, 82
North, Douglass Cecil, 113, 123

O

Ohlin, Bertil, 57–58, 76
Ostrom, Elinor, 136, 137, 146–147
Owen, Robert, 13, 18

P

Phelps, Edmund Strother, 144–145
Phillips curve, 158–159
physiocrats, 5, 10
Pigou, Arthur Cecil, 45–46, 50
Pissarides, Christopher Antoniou, 160, 161, 162, 163, 186–187
Prescott, Edward, 166–167, 180–181
Principles of Economics, 30
Principles of Political Economy and Taxation, 12
prospect theory, 149

R

Ricardo, David, 9–13, 24, 28, 31

S

Samuelson, Paul, 85–86, 89, 98–99, 102, 111
Sargent, Thomas John, 170, 177–179
Schelling, Thomas Crombie, 114–115, 131
Scholes, Myron Samuel, 168–169, 184, 185

Schultz, Theodore William, 69–70, 97
Selten, Reinhard, 109, 129, 133
Sen, Amartya, 140–143
Sharpe, William Forsyth, 119, 127, 150–151
Simon, Herbert Alexander, 100–101
Sims, Christopher Albert, 170–171, 177
Smith, Adam, 1–8, 10, 11, 28, 31, 116
Smith, Vernon, 125–126, 148
Solow, Robert Merton, 121–122
Spence, Michael, 164, 174, 175
Stigler, George Joseph, 84
Stiglitz, Joseph, 164, 174, 175–176
Stone, Sir Richard, 94
supply and demand, 30, 116, 161, 163

T

technocracy, 39
Theory of Moral Sentiments, The, 3, 4, 5–6, 7
Theory of the Leisure Class, The, 36, 37
Tinbergen, Jan, 53, 71–72

Tobin, James, 104–105
Townshend, Charles, 4, 5
trade theory, 57, 58

V

value, theory of, 26, 28, 29, 73
Veblen, Thorstein, 36–40, 43
Vickrey, William, 95–96, 154

W

Walras, Léon, 24–25, 26, 28
welfare economics, 45, 98, 117, 140–141
welfare state, 61
Westphalen, Jenny von, 17, 20–21, 23
Wharton Models, 112
Wicksell, Knut, 35, 58
Wieser, Friedrich von, 32, 34, 59
Williamson, Oliver Eaton, 136–137, 146, 147

Y

Young Hegelians, 16, 17